D0720853

The focus on the person of the Lord Jesus Christ should be every Christian's pursuit and life. Our understanding of His love for us, determines the level reciprocation for which we serve our God. I love Nate as his uncle but admire him even more so for his passion to make much of Christ and to make Him known to others. You will sense his desire to glorify our Lord Jesus throughout these pages."

John Wilkerson
Pastor, First Baptist Church of Hammond

"*Christ Is Life* is a simple and straightforward book that will challenge you to move beyond yourself and walk in total dependence upon the Holy Spirit and radical obedience to His Word."

Pastor Greg Locke
Global Vision Bible Church Mt. Juliet, TN

"*Christ is Life* is refreshingly real. It is transparent and Biblically true in a way that this generation of Christians need and, I believe, is longing for. Wilkerson's love for God is evident in these pages and will inspire you to stand up with him and many other believers around the world to change this world by making Christ your life."

Edward De Los Reyes
Missionary, Vision Baptist Missions

"Nate Wilkerson is a young man with a passion for Christ and a desire to point others to Him. This book reflects that heart. Nate's conversational style of writing and personal experiences will cause you to look at your own heart and ask, "Is Christ my life?" Every young person should read these pages."

Scott Pauley
Evangelist

“At an urgently appropriate time in our history when entire generations have mistakenly equated many variables with this thing we call “life;” Nate presents a compilation of scriptures and stories championing the message that Christ Is Life. This concise resource is a clear roadmap by which anyone can navigate the identity of Christ and His divine purpose. Readers will find their soul stirred by Nate’s authentic passion and their hearts primed by the powerful proof that Christ is life.”

Jon Leighton
Evangelist

“Nate has a passion for people that spurs from his passion and love for Jesus Christ. He exemplifies and displays a life that is led by Christ. In these pages, Nate writes with passion and purpose his love for Jesus. Truly, this book has the potential to change a person’s life forever.”

Jonathan Black
Student Pastor, Southside Baptist Church

“I had the privilege of teaching Nate for a few years, but he continues to teach me. A couple of statements that jumped out at me in this book are these: “God does not exist for us. We exist for Him. Our entire purpose of existence on earth is to glorify God. He does not belong to us. We belong to Him.” I see this lived out in Nate’s life and I am personally challenged to make more of my life do the same. If we would begin living our lives recognizing that “we are not our own” because we are “bought with a price” how much more could we do for the King of Kings and Lord of Lords. As you read this book allow the simplicity of it to overwhelm you in simple obedience to the Word of God.”

Keith Hamilton
Pastor, FHMV Baptist Church

“This book will be a blessing and challenge to all who read it. Nate Wilkerson is a young man whose heart belongs unreservedly to our Saviour, Jesus Christ. It has been a joy to watch his life grow in the Lord since his early teen years. As my grandson, I consider it a wonderful privilege to write this recommendation for his first book, *Christ is Life.* I do believe God will use his young life to impact this generation for Christ! Seldom have I seen the level of commitment that is evident to all who know him. How desperately we need more young men who will follow his example. If one phrase could describe him, it would be a “servant of God” What better could be said of any of us than to be called a servant? Read this book prayerfully and willingly to the glory of God. You and I need a desire to “Make Much Of Jesus” daily in our life to see God use us for His glory!”

Steve Grubbs
Pastor, Gospel Light Baptist Church

CHRIST IS LIFE

Discovering Life in Obedience to God's Will

Nate Wilkerson
with Jacob Clower

All scriptures are taken from The Holy Bible, King James Version.

Cover: Jonathan Black

WestBow Press books may be ordered through booksellers or by contacting:

WestBow Press
A Division of Thomas Nelson & Zondervan
1663 Liberty Drive
Bloomington, IN 47403
www.westbowpress.com
1 (866) 928-1240

ISBN: 978-1-5127-9576-9 (sc)
ISBN: 978-1-5127-9577-6 (hc)
ISBN: 978-1-5127-9575-2 (e)

Library of Congress Control Number: 2017910692

Print information available on the last page.

WestBow Press rev. date: 07/17/2017

Contents

Foreword.......xiii
Acknowledgments.......xvii
Introduction.......xix

Chapter 1 Purpose: What on Earth are We Here for?.......1
- I Once was Lost but Now I'm Found.......6
- The Jesus Christ I Thought I Knew.......8
- The Jesus Christ of the Bible.......10
- Encountering the Real Jesus.......12
- Who is Jesus Christ?.......14
- Challenge.......16

Chapter 2 Priorities: Putting First What Matters Most.......17
- Rich in Finances.......22
- Rich in Family.......23
- Rich in Faith.......26

Chapter 3 Perspective: Learning to See More Like God and Less Like the World.......29
- God's Vision.......33
- Vision of the One True King.......36
- I Once was Blind but Now I see.......47
- Challenge.......49

Chapter 4 Problems: When Things Do Not Go as You Originally Planned 50
Putting God in His Rightful Place 54
God is Not a Dog 55
Why God Gives Us Guidelines 57
Challenge 60

Chapter 5 Patience: Actively Waiting on God's Perfect Timing 61
An Impatient Generation 65
Mind Blown 67
The Mysterious Call 67
Excuses 69
Fear 70
When Helping Actually Hurts 73
Love is Patient 75
Challenge 80

Chapter 6 Purity: Desiring What God Desires........81
You see Worthless, He sees Priceless 84
Challenge 94

Chapter 7 Prayer: Discovering the Power of Talking to God 96
Challenge 109

Chapter 8 Price: What is the Cost of Following Christ? 110
Christ is Worth the Cost 115
Have You Collided with the King? 116
What Does it Mean to Truly Follow Christ? 118
What is God's Will for My Life? 129
God's Will is that We Give Thanks In all Things 131
God's Will is that We Abstain from Sexual Sin .. 133
God's Will is that We Are Actively Involved in Global Evangelism 134

Answering the Tough Questions........................136
Challenge 145

Chapter 9 Persecution: Why Do We Have so Little of What Christ Promised so Much of? 146
How Have We been Persecuted? 151
Revival is a Result of Persecution......................153
How Would You Respond to Persecution? 154
Forgiveness > Judgement................................155
Three Months Before 156
Present Day..160
Challenge 162
The Next Step: The Outpouring of a Life in Christ 163
Thank You 166
About the Author 167
Notes 169
Works Cited 173

"For ye are dead, and your life is hid with Christ in God. When Christ, who is our life, shall appear, then shall ye also appear with him in glory." Colossians 3:3-4

Foreword

> "For to me to live is Christ, and to die is gain." Philippians 1:21

This verse describes Nate Wilkerson. He doesn't just talk about the verse; he lives it out. All who know Nate know that he is contagious, excited, motivated, and on fire for Jesus. He is a young man of great character who truly lives out the meaning of this verse.

Nate can't help but talk about the Lord Jesus Christ and His love for people all over the world. At the age of 18, Nate already has over 45,000 followers on Instagram. His account doesn't promote himself; it promotes Jesus. Nate doesn't seek to promote any personal agenda, just a very outrageous love for God through Jesus Christ. He doesn't miss a beat at trying to get his message out on both social media and in person.

Nate is genuinely concerned about everyone. He wants everyone he meets to know the gospel of Jesus Christ. He has seen people make decisions for Christ from his contact with them on Instagram. He has an infectious love for the Lord Jesus and for you. The words that you are about to read weren't written by someone in an office somewhere thinking about great truths. These words were written by a young man with feet on the ground living life with everyone. Nate has shared his faith with his friends in high school sports. He has shared his faith with people he knows personally and with multiplied thousands that he has never met. He simply wants everyone to know that Christ is life!

This book, or rather the truths taught in this book, can change your life. Nate is an unusual young man but he would say that it is not because of who he is but because of who he knows, the Lord Jesus Christ. Nate is not who he is because of anything in himself. He is who he is because of his personal faith in the Lord Jesus Christ and because of the work that Jesus has done in his life. Nate has life because Nate has Christ. Remember Christ is Life!

Read this book to learn how to know the Lord Jesus as your Savior. Read this book to grow in the grace of the Lord Jesus Christ. Read this book to learn how to share your faith in an effective, contagious way. Life is more than just existing. Life is more than just going through the motions like everyone else. Life is knowing Jesus. Eternal life is about knowing Jesus. Reading this book will help you see how a young man has literally made Philippians 1:21 the true north star of his life. Read the book to see how God just might use you in the same way. You can be used of God to make a difference too. This book was written for you. This book will communicate the truths that changed Nate's life and will change yours, too.

Jesus is not just the answer for Nate Wilkerson's life; He is the answer for all of us. The truth that Christ is life is communicated all through this book. You can have your sins forgiven, your past replaced, and your future secured by knowing Jesus. He will give you a reason to live. The truth of the book is summed up in the title: Christ is Life! Read this book and share it with all of your friends.

My family and I have served God now for over 40 years. We have started and pastored churches in the USA for over 20 years and served as church-planting missionaries in Peru, South America for another 20 years. We have always been trying to do all we can to get the gospel to the world. Nate has done something that literally shocked us. He took his love for Jesus to the internet and began reaching people all over the world. He has effectively shared the gospel and has seen people believe in the Lord Jesus and learn that Christ is life. I want to get the gospel to the world. Nate at such a young age wants to as well and is already being greatly used. You will see that in this book.

Christ is Life is not Nate's story as much as it is the story of Jesus Christ changing lives. Nate is not the hero of this book; rather, he points us to his hero, Jesus, in the pages to follow. Come along on a journey of faith in the Lord Jesus Christ. Watch how God uses a young man to effectively share his faith literally all around the globe.

Austin Gardner
Pastor of Vision Baptist Church
President of Vision Baptist Missions
President of Our Generation Training Center
Alpharetta, Georgia

Acknowledgments

Dozens of people have significantly contributed to making this book possible- from those who have invested their time by offering suggestions, to those who have influenced my life personally. All glory, honor, and praise belongs to Jesus Christ who alone is worthy! I would like to thank all that have taken part in making this dream a reality. I would also like to thank you for taking time to read this.

Special thanks to Jacob Clower who spent many hours with me during the long writing, editing, and review process of this book. If it were not for your dedication to the cause of Christ and commitment to investing hundreds of hours into this manuscript, this book would have many typos and would not be as easy to read. Your selfless effort is invaluable and your Christlike spirit is contagious. I thank the Lord that He saw fit to cross our paths as you have played a vital role in the completion of this manuscript that has the potential to impact many around the world. Thank you does not even begin to describe how deeply I appreciate your love for Christ and desire to get His gospel to the world.

I would also like to thank my loving family for the patience they have graciously bestowed on me throughout this exciting journey. Your encouragement, input, and constructive criticism means more to me than you know. I love each one of you and thank The Lord for you daily.

Introduction

You are not an accident. God created you. He has a great intent and purpose for your life. God loves you and wants to use you to proclaim His love to the world. This is a vital and extremely important truth for the life of every follower of Christ. But you may ask, "How can God use me?" It was not a coincidence that you just happened to come across this book. Everything in your life has taken place for a reason. I am thankful for your willingness to read this book and I hope and pray that it will make an impact in your life. This book can and will change your life if you prayerfully seek the Lord in your efforts for Him.

Follow me on a journey to discover your purpose of existence. Follow me to learn more about God and how to walk in obedience to His will. This book is full of the truth of God's Word. There will be moments while reading where you will be encouraged and uplifted in the Spirit, but there will be other times where you will be convicted. You will be challenged to forsake sin and to pursue Christ. Read these words with an open heart and mind that genuinely seeks to know God deeper and to make Him known to the world. My prayer is that you would not merely read these words and leave the same way you came, but that through the Biblical truths presented, you would discover that there is life found in Christ that is infinitely superior to your wildest imaginations. God desires to use you to reach this world with the gospel of Christ in this generation. I truly believe this and have gone through great lengths to write about the amazing life Christ offers to those who are willing to repent, abandon all, and wholeheartedly follow Him. This book is a call to action. While reading, I want to encourage you to forget everything you think you know. I plead you to take Christ and His commands seriously. Christ is not merely a part of life. He is both the initiator and sustainer of life. Apart from Christ, there is no life. Through the course of this book, we will discover that Christ truly is life.

Chapter 1

Purpose: What on Earth are We Here for?

What is life? There has to be more to life than money, work, and pleasure, yet these often define our lives. Quite frankly, we are selfish. We do not intend to live selfishly, but many times our lives reflect a heart that is filled with our own ambitions. Many Christians today are void of the selfless nature presented by Jesus Christ. You see, the culture we live in screams "do what makes you happy", "follow your heart", "climb and crawl your way up the ladder of success no matter who you step on in the process". The world's agenda has become our agenda. Whether we realize it or not, society is infiltrating our minds, hearts, homes, communities, and nations. Is this really the life that God intended for Christians?

Why are we here on earth? What is the purpose of our existence? Are we merely mistakes of nature that exist only to fulfill our own wants, needs, and desires? Or is there a higher purpose to this thing called life? These are just a few questions I have heard countless times and the answer is actually quite simple. God has a purpose intended for each and every person that has ever lived and will ever live on earth. God created us because He is love. Love is an action verb and hence, it must be acted upon. God, who is love, created us as objects to receive His love. Our purpose is to know God and to make Him known. This is why we exist. This is the reason we are alive. Christ is life.

Our self-centered mentality is the driving force of our identity and the purpose of our actions. This was never the way God intended us to live. God has a purpose for us is far beyond our finite imaginations. God created you and me to glorify Him alone. God designed us in such a way that we will only find the everlasting satisfaction we desperately desire in a relationship with His Son, Jesus Christ. Life is not contingent upon what we do, say, or think, but on who Christ is and what He has done. In and of ourselves we are nothing and can achieve nothing of any lasting value. However, through Christ, we can be used to accomplish extraordinary things that far exceed our expectations. For instance, imagine a band attempting a performance during halftime at a football game. Only this band is without a conductor. Each musician is playing his or her favorite song. Each one of them is doing what he or she wants and what sounds right in his or her own eyes. The sound is horrendous. There is no order or unity; only chaos. In a similar way, when each individual does what he or she believes is right, it leads to confusion and discouragement for followers of Christ. You see, living for ourselves only leaves us empty and desiring more. You will never be satisfied until you encounter the only source of true, everlasting satisfaction in Jesus Christ.

The Word of God contains many examples of distraction, discouragement, and destruction as a direct result of selfishness. The children of Israel did what was right in their own eyes. They sinned. God recompensed them according to their disobedience. One such instance in Joshua 7 and 8 tells us the story of a man who directly disobeyed the command of God. The Lord had promised to deliver Jericho into the hands of the children of Israel. I am sure that most of you have heard the story of the Israelites marching around the city of Jericho and the walls coming down. God gave the children of Israel a command that they were not to touch anything for the city was cursed. God gives clear instructions to refrain from taking anything in the city.[1] The Lord instructed that anything possessing value was consecrated unto the Lord and was to be put into the treasury of the Lord.

The chosen people of God obeyed His instruction and destroyed the city. The Lord brought a great victory as He promised. The fame of Jericho's fall was echoed throughout all the land. However, this victory was short lived due to the disobedience of one man. One of the Israelites named Achan disobeyed God by stealing something from the city. The anger of the Lord was kindled against the children of Israel. When Israel went up to take out the city of Ai, 36 men died. This loss of life and devastating defeat of the battle for Ai was a direct result of Achan's single selfish act in disobedience to God's command. Joshua and the elders of Israel, distraught and confused, humbled themselves before the Lord by tearing their clothes and falling on their faces before the Lord. They put dust upon their heads and sought guidance from the Lord. Joshua then questioned why the Lord would do such a thing to His great name. The Lord responded by telling Joshua to get off his face and find the one who sinned by stealing of what He had consecrated unto Himself. They found Achan, who confessed to stealing a garment, silver, and gold from Jericho. As a result of the sin Achan committed against God and the Israelites, God commanded that Achan and all of his possessions, including his family, be stoned and burned. God undoubtedly had a great purpose for Achan and his family, but sin happened. Achan chose to sin against God instead of following His commandment. The result is death and destruction not only for Achan but also for his entire family and the lives of 3 dozen soldiers.

In the sad story of Achan's disobedience we learn one very important lesson; the result of sin is not limited only to Achan's life. Achan's sin ultimately ended the life of his family as well. Wow. Next time you are tempted to sin think of this story. Would you be more or less likely to sin if you knew the consequences would affect your loved ones? If you knew that your sin could bring about the pain and death of your spouse, children, mother, father, or friends would you be more likely to resist temptation and flee? Remember the long arm of sin can reach into every part of our lives and wreak havoc. Purpose in your heart today to acknowledge the deadly effect of sin and flee it. Surely if Achan were here today he would advise each of us that sin is not worth it. Sin will take you farther than you ever intended to go, keep you longer than you ever intended to stay, and cost you infinitely more than you ever intended to pay. Daily decide to trade the temporary pleasures of sin for the everlasting satisfaction found in obedience to Christ.

Perhaps you have perceived the incoming corruption that selfishness brings and wonder what you can do about it. How you can protect yourself and your families from being polluted? How you can warn others from being morphed into the world's selfish way of thinking? Living for ourselves will only leave us empty and void of joy and peace. Deep down we know that there is something more. That something is actually Someone named Jesus Christ; He is the only one who can completely satisfy your soul and give you a purpose that is beyond all selfish desire. You were not created to please yourself. You were created for a much greater purpose than achieving temporary accomplishments, fulfilling selfish desires, and building a kingdom that will one day pass away. In the following pages we will study a man who successfully defied the world's philosophies and did something no king in history has ever done before. As we take an inside look into the life of the greatest man who ever walked on the face of the earth, we will discover the secret to finding the illuminating light, unconditional love, and everlasting satisfaction that our souls desperately desire.

I Once was Lost but Now I'm Found

I was driving to go see a friend of mine when I suddenly lost my cell phone reception. Now you have to understand that my cell phone was my sole source of direction. I saw before I lost service that my turn was twenty more miles away, but after driving about a dozen or so miles, I was getting worried. I was worried that I missed the turn and was going in the wrong direction. I was far away from home in a location unknown to me without a guide and without any direction. I was genuinely scared for my life. I know that might sound a bit extreme, but without that source of comfort, I felt completely reliant on my sense of direction which was very limited. Like Peter while walking on the water, I temporarily took my eyes off of Jesus and directed my attention to my problem and sunk into a sea of fear and worry.

Whether you can relate directly or have been lost in another way before, I am sure that you have experienced the gut-wrenching feeling of being in a completely helpless state. When we get in a hopeless situation, such as the example above, our focus shifts. Typically our focus adheres to the idea of how we can get out of the troubling situation. The focus shifts to the problem. How can we get this problem to go away? In cases like mine on the road, I had no other options. I immediately turned to the One of whom I asked for a safe trip that I decided to go on. I neglected to ask Him for approval of my choice to temporarily leave my family. God showed me that I am nobody and can accomplish nothing apart from Him. I merely asked Him to bless my decision. Isn't this, many times, what we do when we encounter trials? As followers of Christ, is this right? I believe that the purpose of Christ's disciples is to always trust God and get His approval for all of our actions.

Many times the Lord wants us to focus solely on Him and realize that He alone is enough. Sometimes this requires the Father to allow His children to go through uncomfortable situations. It's sort of like the way children act when they get close to someone. I often preach in children's church and when I tell the children to do something, they typically smart off to me by saying "No", or asking "Why should we obey you?" in a sarcastic tone. So to cure this problem I decided to give them positive incentives. I offered a grand prize of 1 entire dollar to the boy or girl who was sitting up the straightest, listening the best, and being the quietest. This initially worked like a charm. I instantly gained the respect, obedience, and approval of the children. This, however, while it still motivated the large majority to do right, left a few trouble-making kids feeling like they could not even win if they tried. After the same couple of kids kept winning week after week, slowly, but surely, most of them lost interest in trying to do the right thing as they felt like they were attempting to win at a lost cause.

We had to think of another incentive that would drive all of the children, even the naturally rebellious ones, to respectfully obey. We had to remove them from their comfort zones in order to get them to realize who really had the authority and rule during the service. I was forced to have to take them out of what was comfortable in order to get them to see that I was in charge. God often does the same thing. He wants Christ's love to constrain us to obey Him so that we can find true joy in willingly submitting to and obeying the will of the Father. God is love. He loves us and wants to give us good gifts. He wants to be the only provider of our needs and desires. He wants us to find joy and satisfaction in freely submitting to His commands. Only when we get distracted and full of pride to the extent that we attempt to "live life on our own" is He forced to allow us to go through difficulties in order for us to see that "He is and He is the rewarder of them that diligently seek Him."[2]

The Jesus Christ I Thought I Knew

Growing up I always perceived Jesus as a kind, long-haired, loving guy. You know, the Sunday school lessons about His loving and forgiving nature. The more I heard, the more I began to perceive the Jesus I thought I knew as a hippy on the side of the road instead of the King who reigns in my heart. I began to see Jesus as Someone who could please me. "This is awesome!" I thought, "I can sin all I want and then just ask for forgiveness and it's as if I never sinned in the first place!" "Forgive me." "Comfort me." "Heal me."

"Protect me." "Love me." "Give me." "Bless me." These are a few of the demands that consumed all of my prayers. All I thought of was myself; it was all about me. Yet, as great as this sounds, and sounded to me at the time, this is not our purpose as followers of Christ and we will be miserable if we attempt to fit Jesus into a box that we create. Christ, like a consuming fire, cannot be contained.

I was living a selfish life and expecting Jesus to contribute to making my life better for me. I felt an empty void deep in my soul. I thought, "Is this what life feels like as a disciple of Jesus?" I started doubting my salvation. I prayed a prayer. I got baptized. I went to church. I even read the Bible more than all of my friends. I questioned God saying, "Why do I feel so alone?" "Where are you?" "If you exist, prove it!" I decided to study for myself if this "truth" I had been raised up believing *really* was the truth.

I began this journey by studying the Bible. I read the words of Jesus and sought to apply them to my life by living in obedience to His instruction. I started circling every command Christ gave and really attempted to obey each and every one. I fell short. It seemed like the more I strove to obey this new Jesus, the more I found myself unable to comply with His requests. Unlike the Jesus I thought I knew, this newfound Jesus I studied for myself in God's Word actually asked something of me. He gave me unachievable tasks to accomplish and expected me to succeed. I learned that it was impossible for me to adequately comply with every command in my own strength. The Jesus I thought I knew never asked anything of me. In fact, my "relationship" with Christ consisted primarily of me asking things of Him. The Jesus I am now following is much different and far better than the phony version of Him that I had created in my imagination. The true Jesus Christ that I discovered by studying the Word of God is the Jesus Christ of the Bible.

The Jesus Christ of the Bible

Two thousand years ago a virgin conceived of the Holy Ghost and bare a son. This baby was unique. He was unlike any that had ever been on earth and there would never be another like Him. He would revolutionize the world by doing something that had never been done before. He would defy the laws of man to proclaim the laws of God. Thousands of people followed Jesus because of His many, mighty miracles. Jesus healed the sick, gave sight to the blind, made the lame walk, made the dumb talk, and even brought the dead to life. John 21:25 tells us that only part of Jesus' actions are told. It says that if all were told then the entire earth could not contain all of the books that should be written. Thousands came to Christ for physical healing, but Christ truly came to give spiritual healing. Through Christ, people who only knew hate learned forgiveness. Jesus Christ knew no sin and willingly chose to become sin for all humanity.

He would cause those who knew only hate to forgive. He would make the dead to live. He would give His life a ransom for many. He who knew no sin would willingly choose to become sin for us. He surrendered to the Father's will above His own and drank the entirety of the wrath towards sin that was reserved for us. He would become the one and only way to Heaven. He would suffer unimaginable torture as he watched the hands of men that He delicately created hammer nails through His hands and feet.

He would ask the Father to forgive those who ignorantly mocked the God-man who left the comfort of Heaven so that all could inherit everlasting life through Him. He who originated life would breathe His final breath and die, but not even death could hold Him. He rose from the dead. Death would lose its clutches on the Life Giver and everlasting life would be freely available to anyone who would repent of their sins and trust in Christ alone for salvation.

This was the plan for the life of Jesus Christ, but for His work on the cross to be completed then He had to survive during the most vulnerable years of His life- His infancy. Satan desired nothing more than to stop this work before it began. This enemy used a man named King Herod to attempt the murder of the innocent young Messiah long before He had the opportunity to accomplish the will of God. God's will for Christ's life was to be born of a virgin, convict sin, expose truth, die for the sins of the world, rise from the dead, and ascend once again to Heaven from where He came. The evil one wanted to destroy the Son of God who would one day destroy him, but his plan failed. The devil has a will for your life and if you are doing his will then you are not doing God's will. There is no middle ground. The enemy does not want you to know God's will for he knows that if he can keep you from knowing the will of God, then he can keep you from doing it.

Ultimately, Jesus Christ accomplished the Father's will by dying for the sin of every person past, present, and future. Three days later, Christ rose from the dead forever signifying His glorious power over sin and death. Those who repent of their sins and place their complete trust in Christ alone for salvation will receive everlasting life through Him. When we have an understanding of who Jesus Christ really is, we are in a position to discover who we really are.

Encountering the Real Jesus

The following testimony is an example of a young lady named Avery who initially decided to take her life into her own hands. She had given away something that she could never get back. She was pressured by her boyfriend, and after months of resisting, she consented. Avery felt dirty. She had acted in the moment and placed herself in the wrong situation at the wrong time with the wrong person. She had no father or male role model in the picture and desperately desired more than anything to be loved, cherished, and cared about. In order to feel that way, she lowered her standards because of impatience and she continually carries the load of guilt today.

Avery's story is similar to millions of girls all around the world. But, unlike the numerous others, her story does not end there. Avery continued seeking something-anything that would complete her, and provide her with the everlasting satisfaction she so desperately desired. She started going to a Bible study at school where she heard the true gospel for the first time. Now, you have to understand that Avery was just as much of a "Christian" as anyone else at the school. Avery read the "verse of the day" as it came across her phone each morning. She always thought of how pleased God must be with her for reading that verse each day. Avery also prayed to God for help every time she was in trouble. Sometimes Avery would even go to church with her friends to ease her conscience. Avery knew that God was good, but like the vast majority of the students at her school she was unsaved. Avery served her own god; she did not know the Jesus of the Bible.

One week at the Bible study, a crazy guy got up to preach about something that she, along with a good ninety percent of the others, had never heard. This fanatical preacher preached something so different, so dangerous, and so mysteriously irresistible that you could hear a pin drop in the room. This passionate stranger quoted words of Jesus that had scarcely been preached. "Jesus requires more than a couple hours a week and a couple minutes a day. Jesus calls those who truly wish to follow Him to abandon all. The Christ of the Bible says that His followers must completely and unreservedly relinquish every ambition, dream, goal, thought, and desire to His control." She was in shock. Tears began to stream down her face as she realized that this same Christ that had sacrificed everything for her was asking her to surrender her life to Him. She wept silently at the thought of her selfishness, fear, and blatant rebellion that had caused her to do unspeakable things. That morning Avery claims to have come to a saving knowledge of the Jesus Christ of the Bible.

Avery is a real girl that went to my high school. She has made many mistakes as have we all, but Avery decided, against the odds, to follow the Jesus of the Bible. She has far to go, but is growing deeper in her relationship with Jesus and learning more with every passing day. Avery has learned that Jesus is all she needs, and she wants everyone to know who this Jesus is.

Who is Jesus Christ?

Who is Jesus Christ? Wow! That's the most loaded question I have ever attempted to answer! I realize that I cannot adequately provide an answer to this question. I am not qualified to describe the Son of God therefore, I will list some verses below that Jesus speaks to describe himself.

John 14:6 "Jesus saith unto him, I am the way, the truth, and the life: no man cometh unto the Father, but by me."

John 6:35 "And Jesus said unto them, I am the bread of life: he that cometh to me shall never hunger; and he that believeth on me shall never thirst."

John 8:12 "Then spake Jesus again unto them, saying, I am the light of the world: he that followeth me shall not walk in darkness, but shall have the light of life."

John 10:9 "I am the door: by me if any man enter in, he shall be saved, and shall go in and out, and find pasture."

John 10:11 "I am the good shepherd: the good shepherd giveth his life for the sheep."

The Jesus Christ of the Bible is much different than the way we perceive Him. He is not some long haired hippy as He is often portrayed in pictures. He is not some imaginary companion that we can use and abuse to gratify our own desires by taking advantage of His grace. Whether you believe it or not, millions all around the world see Jesus as nothing more than a crutch. This is not who Jesus is. Those who treat Him as such, have no understanding of who He is, why He died, and why He lives.

Jesus Christ came to convince those who thought of themselves to be saints that they are sinners in need of the Savior. He came to make the seeing blind and the blind see. He came to transform sinners into saints. This is why He came. But who is He?

First off, we must come to a consensus that, based on His own words, Christ is the Son of God. Agreed? Good. This is vital because if He is not God, He is nothing more than a mere man. Anyone can claim to be anything, but if proven actions cannot confirm that one is who they claim to be, they are merely words. In addition, many have even claimed to be the Christ, but none of these were able to do the things Jesus did. Some still argue that Christ was only a man, a prophet, a zealous fanatic that came, attempted to overthrow Rome, and was crucified never to be seen again. However, both historical and scientific evidence has proven Him to have been dead and risen from the dead this means that this professed Son of God was exactly who He claimed to be.

As the true Son of God, Jesus naturally made a great name for Himself. Jesus Christ is the single most influential person to have ever walked the face of earth. There has never been nor will there ever be another person like Jesus Christ. He alone sits as the supreme Ruler of all. He is far more than words could ever describe or thoughts could ever conceive. Regardless of what people think or say, one day every knee will bow and every tongue confess that Jesus Christ is Lord to the glory of God the Father.[3] I could go on forever and fill ten-thousand pages up in an attempt to describe The Indescribable One, but Christ claims and proves that He is God He is The Great I AM.

Challenge

In light of who Christ is, what steps can we take to become more like Him? How can we adjust our lives to more effectively magnify Christ? In what ways can we reflect His light with those within our sphere of influence? Who is truly the one I am seeking to please, glorify, and make much of? Which areas of my life need to be surrendered completely to Christ's control? If those who know me do not know Christ, then how can I claim that Christ is my life? If Christ returned in the next day, what would I have to offer Him as a gift for offering Himself for me?

Chapter 2

Priorities: Putting First What Matters Most

What matters most? What is of the greatest importance? Priorities are the most misplaced things in all the world. Priorities are misplaced because we are naturally inclined to think of ourselves first. We care about others, but typically only after we have everything we need and desire first and foremost. Every human being is born with this mentality because of our sin nature. Once Christ truly saves us, His desires will start to become our desires. When Christ becomes our life, He puts to death our sin nature and creates in us a new nature. We will then find ourselves thinking of Him and His will for us rather than our own. As Christ's desires become our desires, we will slowly but surely begin to desire to help others before we help ourselves. This is love. God is love.[1] The closer we get to God, the more we will love. Love is putting the needs of others above the needs of ourselves. With all of the right intentions, we often settle to put God in the back seat of our lives. He is not the true priority.

One hot summer day, a woman left her two-year-old son in her car while she went to do some shopping. As soon as she returned, she was appalled to find her keys were locked in her car with her son. She immediately called the authorities who insisted that since the temperature was 88 degrees, they break her window to free the child and save his life. She, not willing to damage her 1999 Audi, had the audacity to look them in the face and say "no." She, understanding the severity of the situation decided to compromise and borrow someone's car to get an extra pair of keys at her house about 5 minutes away. While she was gone, the firefighters broke her window and the paramedics helped the unresponsive child regain consciousness. When the woman returned several minutes later she was arrested for reckless endangerment and risk of injury to a minor. She later claimed that the reason she did not want the window broken was because she was worried that the glass would hurt her son. Either way, this woman loved her son, but she evidently loved her car more and was willing to place her son in risk of heat stroke and possible death for the sake of a car.

This is one example of an insane case of misplaced priorities. But many times, if we are being completely honest with ourselves, we act in a similar way towards God. Our lives represent the car. There is something far more valuable inside that, whether we realize or not, we love less than the appearance of ourselves. We love God, do not get me wrong. We just love ourselves and the way other people perceive us more. We do not like to admit that because our social media profiles say "God first" and we generally put Him as a high priority. But He is not first place. Like the woman wanting to get closer to her son, we want to get closer to God. But rarely do we desire to be close to Him at our expense. We are worried that if we actually do what it takes to get closer to Him, people will look at us as "different." What will it take to be genuinely close to The Father? The avenue to intimacy with the Father is brokenness. It will require that we break some things in our lives. In the same way that a glow stick must first be broken in order to shine, God's children must first go through periods of brokenness in order to illuminate Christ's light in a dark world. We will be looked at differently because our priorities are different. We will stand out from all the other outwardly "perfect" exhibitions that people put on because we live for a different purpose.

Being completely willing to do what it takes to be close to The Lord takes sacrifice, denial, and commitment that few are willing to surrender to. Is being close to your Heavenly Father truly worth the "sacrifice" of our entire lives? Yes. Pride, fear, anger, resentment, doubt, self-pity, and unbelief are just a few of the sins I attempted to harbor inside for a time. I lived a life of outward success and prosperity while inwardly I was living in constant defeat. I can tell you from experience that choosing to exchange my sins for Christ is the single most important decision I have ever made. Immediately after I traded all of me for all of Him, I received and unexplainable peace that a very small percent of people will ever experience. It is incredible. I am constantly full of joy. I desire solely to *know Christ deeper* so that I can *make Him known* to the nations in the most effective way. In Christ alone resides everlasting satisfaction. Christ alone can provide the eternal fulfillment that our hungry hearts desperately desire, but we can only discover Him by denying our desires and ambitions.

I like the example that C.S Lewis gives in his book, *The Weight of Glory* when comparing the difference between what we settle for and what we can have in Christ:

> "If we consider the unblushing promises of reward and the staggering nature of the rewards promised in the Gospels, it would seem that Our Lord finds our desires not too strong, but too weak. We are half-hearted creatures, fooling about with drink and sex ambition when infinite joy is offered us, like an ignorant child

> who wants to go on making mud pies in a slum because he cannot imagine what is meant by the offer of a holiday at the sea. We are far too easily pleased..."

The problem is not that we desire too strongly, but that we are content settling for something of far less satisfaction. It is like eating a public school chicken sandwich when a Chick-fil-a chicken sandwich is only a few steps away. We have become so lazy that we are unwilling to get that which is incomparably better merely because it requires effort and we will have to give up what we think to be too valuable. We, like the Laodicean church, have free access to all the wonderful things God desires to give us. These people say, "I am rich, and increased with goods, and have need of nothing."[2] These people were ignorant of their worth in the sight of Almighty God. His standard for our lives is much greater than we can even fathom, but since we do not place God as the top priority then we will always be blind. God uses the words "wretched, and miserable, and poor, and blind, and naked" to describe the lukewarm people of this church that very closely resembles America. The Almighty then tells them that He advises them to buy gold from Him that has been tried in the fire and is without spot so that they can truly be rich. He also has an abundance of white raiment to cover the shame of their nakedness. Christ alone possesses the ability to heal the blindness of all those who fail to put God as the top priority in our lives.

Rich in Finances

The Laodicean Church mentioned in Revelation chapter 3 was a wealthy group of people. Similarly as the Laodicean people, we today, especially Americans, are filthy rich. Many times we do not like to admit this truth, nevertheless in comparison with the world we are extremely wealthy. The majority of the world makes an average of 2 dollars a day. We, as Americans are amongst the wealthiest people on planet earth. The Lord has given me the opportunity to travel overseas on multiple missions trips, and one evident fact is that in the eyes of the world we are considered rich. I have witnessed various individuals literally walk over a one dollar bill at a Walmart. Whether on purpose or accidentally, they neglected to make the effort to stop, reach down and pick up half the salary of one days hard work for the majority of souls in the world.

Now you may be thinking "I would never do that." Me neither, but the fact of the matter is that if you have this book in your hand, you are far wealthier than most people. God considers the many of the rich of this world "poor" and many of the poor of this world "rich." He beckons those who He has blessed with monetary wealth to abandon our right to it and be willing to use it to assist those who are going into all the world to preach the gospel to every creature.

I was 14 years old and the owner of my own small landscaping company. I was my own boss. I would occasionally hire either my brother or another worker for additional help on busy days, but I typically did everything myself. I was making plenty of money which gave me quite a dilemma. Initially I struggled with giving to God. I worked tirelessly for the money

I had and although I inwardly knew God deserved that which He gave me the power and capability to attain, but for some reason it was still difficult at first. As I was studying the Word of God, I was repetitively convicted and compelled to give in abundance to the wonderful God who had so abundantly given to me. I was surprised to find that however much I gave, I received exactly twice that amount in less than a day after I gave it. You see, God owns this world. He has riches untold and desires to freely bestow them to His obedient children. We are the ones who, many times, shorten God's hand.

Determine this day to relinquish complete control of every cent God has given you the ability to attain and everything he allows you to make in the future solely for the advancement of Christ's kingdom. God does not need or want your money; He wants your heart. He wants to bless you abundantly if you are willing to love Him enough to obey Him. You will never regret giving back to God a portion of what He has given to you. Money is merely a tool to get the Gospel to the world.

Rich in Family

I realize that there are many that have broken families. One night there was a bus kid who ran into the woods behind the church immediately after the service. As soon as I was informed, I ran after him and tried to get him to calm down by listening to him tell me through tears and sobs about his broken family. His cousin lived with the family for several years and was very abusive to him. He told me that his cousin would often beat him with a metal pole until he was black and blue. He told me stories of his cousin doing everything from throw bricks at his head for fun to shooting him in one of his limbs to make him "tougher". His dad was his only source of solace. One day, he woke up only to find his father lying unresponsive on the floor where he had taken his life. He was devastated. His only source of comfort, the only one he loved was gone. He wept in bitter despair for days. He had no known family except his step brother. With nothing to lose, he went to try his luck at their house. There he found his birth-mother. She busted out in tears at the sight of him. She told him how his father took him away from her in the middle of the night when she slept and how she searched for them for 3 years until she finally all but gave up hope.

Between sobs, he expounded upon how when he was younger, he was hit by his school bus driver and spent several months in the hospital with few and often no visitors. Looking deep into my eyes, he explained how just a few hours before church, his little brother put a gun in his mouth and told him that nobody loved him. His brother then told him that since he spared his life by not killing him, he owed him his life. Forsaken, abandoned, isolated, and lonely were words he used to describe the way he was feeling. He kept sobbing uncontrollably and punching trees as he walked recklessly toward an upcoming cliff. I was in shock. Never in all my life had I heard so many insane things happen to one person in only 17 years of life. I told him the only thing I knew to say, "God is your loving Heavenly Father. He cares about you and has a plan for your life and a purpose for the pain you are going through."

At this point he was screaming questions at me such as "Why would a loving God allow all of these terrible things to happen to me?" and "What did I do to deserve such a difficult life?" I was genuinely choked up and tears began streaming down my face as I told him "I don't know." I continued, "We can't always understand why God allows certain things to happen and why He does what He does. We must simply trust that He has a plan that is far beyond our wildest imaginations." I persisted, "Perhaps God put you through this because He desires to use you as a beacon of hope for others that have gone through similar situations." After hours of talking, the Lord used His Word to convince him that Christ alone was worth living for, and that God was his loving Heavenly Father. My friend learned that it did not matter what other people said or thought about him. His Heavenly Father of love was the only approval that he needed and sought after.

No matter if your family background is similar to this story or not, God loves you deeply. Maybe you are blessed to have a family in a local, Bible believing church. There are many fellow believers that the Father has rescued from a sinful path headed toward certain destruction just like He did for you. No matter where you have been or what you have gone through, there is a loving God who loves you with an eternal love. There are people who have been loved by God and, in return, seek to show his love to others. The church is not a museum for saints, but a hospital for the broken. The church's primary goal ought to be glorifying God by actively obeying the commands that Christ gave.

We are rich in family, if for no other reason, because we have access to Christ's church where we can be encouraged in love by saints.

Rich in Faith

America is the wealthiest country in the world when it comes to how much access we have to the Gospel. I grew up in the heart of what is considered by many "the Bible belt." In the 10 minute drive to church we would pass at least twenty churches that were visible from the road. eighteen out of the twenty were Bible believing and preaching churches all within a 2 miles. At my current church, I know of at least 40 Bible believing churches within a 5 mile radius. This is much different from a city I recently visited on a missions trip. Arequipa, Peru is a city most have never heard of. There are currently around 2 million souls living there with little to no access of the Gospel. When many American Christians hear of the country Peru, they consider it "reached." I have been there. I have stood amidst a small group of both American and Peruvian Christians in a Catholic cemetery. Tears were flowing from the missionary as he took us to 3 small graves of three young children. The missionary sadly spoke of the 3 graves saying that "These could very likely be the only 3 in Heaven as they, unlike these other thousands, had not reached the age of accountability." We walked all throughout the place wondering "if only the gospel had gotten here sooner they might not have perished."

There are around 30 Bible preaching churches in the city of Arequipa, but let's be generous and say there's 50. When you divide the population of 2 million by 50, which equals 40,000. It would take each church to reach 40,000 souls with the gospel for Arequipa to be reached. This is the most evangelized city in the entire country. There is an overwhelming need for the gospel around the world. While there is a need in America, the need outside America is exponentially higher. About 95% of the world lives outside of America while only a measly 5% are contained within. 95% of Bible college graduates stay within 5% of the world while 5% go to the 95%. When my missionary friend shared this with me at a restaurant, it changed my entire perspective on just how backwards we are about accomplishing the great commission. In America we are rich in our access to the gospel of Jesus Christ, but this is not true in all countries around the world.

Christ's last command ought to be our first priority. While we enjoy the comforts of heating and air-conditioning, running water, abundance of delicious food and water, there are millions who are without such convenient accommodations. While we have the ability to go to church 1, 2, and even 3 times a week and sit in cushioned chairs, Chinese believers are packed like sardines into small, undercover buildings to meet in "secret church". While the only risk most of us take is the possibility of being pulled over for speeding to get to church on time, there are thousands who risk their occupations, reputations, and even lives for the sake of Christ. They genuinely believe that hearing from God's Word is worth the risk. They love God and they are living examples that prove what complete abandonment truly looks like. Yet even while the numbers of "secret" Christians in countries where religious freedom is unknown, there are still so many who have not yet heard. We are rich in faith in America with the ability to attend church and live our lives in the way we please, but there are so many who do not have this opportunity. They are poor in faith, they are poor in the gospel, but they still need to know. Who is going to tell them? As we change our priorities to reflect Christ then we will really serve Him. Sometimes our perspective keeps us from seeing truth.

In comparison, we often regard that being unfriended and unfollowed because we have the words "God first" or "I love God", a sacrifice and persecution. Most of us have no clear conception of what reckless abandon to Jesus really looks like. For those who have seen it and strive to live in obedience, there is a notable difference in their lives. I challenge you to put down the temporary trinkets this world has offered and distracted us with, and choose to surrender all to Christ alone.

Chapter 3

Perspective: Learning to See More Like God and Less Like the World

The Lord had given me the opportunity to go on a missions trip to Peru and I was filled with uncontainable joy! As we headed to the airport, my mind was filled with a curiosity that cannot really be explained in words. I had never been to an airport before and seeing all these planes flying in and out was nothing short of incredible to me. Excitement filled the air like a cool breeze on a warm summer night. After waiting impatiently for several hours, it was finally time to board the plane. We anxiously anticipated the coming days, not knowing what an impact they were going to have on our lives. I knew this trip had the potential to add purpose to my life like never before, but I could have never imagined the life-altering influence that seeing a world blindly walking into a Christ-less eternity could have in my life.

As soon as we arrived in Lima and got into a van, we discovered that traffic laws were merely a suggestion and rarely enforced. As a result, they were rarely obeyed. Needless to say, it felt as if we barely made it to the hotel in one piece. The brief, yet exhilarating, experience instantly brought my mind into curiosity of how dangerously disoriented the life of a Christian would be without the enforcer of God's Word. I breathed a sigh of relief as I discovered we were staying in one of the most luxurious hotels in Lima. However, it was 2 o'clock in the morning and seeing as we were to fly out from Lima to Arequipa the following morning, I decided to try to get some sleep. I woke up 3 short hours later with a flood of adventurous curiosity that overwhelmed my soul. I started reading the Bible and did so with a renewed sense of animation. There were thousands of thoughts running through my head.

I smelled unique Peruvians fragrances, heard peculiar Peruvian sounds, tasted exclusive Peruvian food, and witnessed beautiful Peruvian people who seemed to have a hunger to know truth and desperately sought the way to Heaven. I was amazed with the Peruvian people. Their kindness, generosity, and contentment was both an exciting and refreshing break from the typical American mundane apathy of so many Americans. Unable to contain all the new smells, sounds, flavors, feelings, and emotions within me, I decided to start writing down as such as I could so that I could go back later and revisit these wonderful memories. I became more aware of the fact that the need to get the gospel to the world is desperately more urgent than I knew. It was of highest necessity to Christ that the world hear the gospel. Therefore, it should be the top priority of everyone who claims to follow Him. And as I learned more and more about the world outside of America then the more my perspective shifted away from the American ideals of complacency and apathy.

By spending multiple hours examining the scriptures, it became abundantly clear to me that world evangelism was never intended by Jesus to be merely "a part" or "a ministry" of the church. We find that world evangelism, how Christ designed it, is to be both the foundation on which the church is built and the purpose for its existence. It is obvious that Jesus had compassion on the lost multitudes and desired that all would be saved. In fact, we see in Mark 15:16 that it was of so much importance that the last recorded words of Christ were, "Go ye into all the world and preach the gospel to every creature." This very last command of Christ to "Go" should be the first priority of every Christian in the world! There is reasonable evidence to believe that the last words of the risen Son of the Living God are undeniably of utmost importance. Every follower of Christ should have a burden for the lost and dying world. Sometimes a priority shift can only occur through a renewed perspective of the entire lost and dying world outside of one's own county.

Having been overseas and having seen the need, I am in awestruck wonder at how amazing our God is to take those with "no hope" and transform them into some of the most hope-filled individuals on planet earth. I have witnessed souls who were once lost sinners encounter the Christ of the Bible in such a radical way that transformed their hate into love, their bitterness into forgiveness, and their selfish desire into selfless action. The desire to live in enmity with God is gone from the lives of these people. Christ changed them! He renewed their perspectives to the eternal rather than the temporary. They now desire to live for Christ and share Him with all people. They devoted their lives to Christ after their encounter with Him. You may be wondering, "How did this happen?" "What did these believers get about Jesus that I am lacking?" Perhaps you want the same difference to take place in your life? The answer to the question you are seeking is found in the Word of God.

God's Vision

John 3:16 "For God so loved the world that He gave His only begotten son that whosoever believeth in Him should not perish, but have everlasting life."

God's vision is a world vision. He desires for the entire world to hear the Gospel and to be saved. In order to see the world as God sees it, we must broaden our perspectives. Nothing will give you a completely renewed perspective like going overseas on a missions trip. I remember my first overseas missions trip to Peru. It totally transformed my outlook on life from local to global.

I stopped seeing others as merely bodies, and started seeing them as souls that will one day spend an eternity in either Heaven or Hell. I started talking to people. I soon came to the realization of the fact that there are thousands of souls walking with the blindfold of religion into a Christ-less eternity. I have spoken with real people who genuinely believe that they are on their way to Heaven when their salvation is based upon something they have done. Salvation is not a goal to be achieved, but a gift to be received by faith in Jesus Christ. Many people like the made up version of Jesus that they have created in their minds. The comfortable Jesus is attractive to a world who wants something from Him and desires to do very little for Him. You see, most proclaimed "Christians" live peaceful, easy, and happy lives. They suffer very little persecution because they are no threat to the enemy. We will learn more about persecution and its effects in the chapter about Persecution.

This is not true Christianity. This is a cheap Christianity with little cost and it will be rewarded with a cheap crown to lay at the feet of the Savior. I do not know about you, but I want to lay down as much as possible at Christ's feet in return for all that He has done for me. I do not want to be empty handed before The Potentate One. Tomorrow, if The Lord saw fit to take you home, or returned to receive His saints, and you stood face to face before Him, what would you have to show for the time, blessings, and opportunities that He has given you? Grab hold of this vision and perspective of who Christ really is and who you really are in Him!

There is a world that is desperately seeking love, satisfaction, and peace. What they are really seeking is Jesus Christ. He alone provides the unconditional love, everlasting satisfaction, and indescribable peace that many seek yet few find. There are some blindfolded by their own lusts and ambitions and will willingly reject the Gospel. But there are also those who, like the Ethiopian eunuch, who are eager to find the truth, but cannot understand unless someone cares enough to obey Christ's command to go and tell them of the wonderful love we have received.

It is no surprise to anyone that we live in an obviously fallen world. From racism to violence, the world we live in is dark and growing darker with every passing day. Selfishness is the perspective of the world, but Christ calls His followers to be selfless and apart from the world. I have heard people tell me that they would kill someone for $1,000. Furthermore, I have been threatened to the extent that the person threatening me vividly described how he was going to kill me. If there is one thing I have been made aware of, it is the fact that we live in a wicked world that is full of those who seek their own vain glory and temporary pleasure. It has once been said that "the darker the night, the brighter the stars shine". How true that is!

There was a sermon illustration that I saw once that perfectly depicted just how much light illuminates the darkness. The preacher turned off all the lights in the room and lit a single candle. Everyone in the large building could see the light piercing the darkness. He then told us to reach under our chairs and grab a little candle and hold it up. He then lit each candle on the front row and instructed them to light the candles to the left and right. In a matter of minutes, every candle was lit in the entire auditorium. Moments before the entire room was in utter darkness, but after every candle was lit it was more illuminated than ever before.

When Christ sets someone on fire, it is His intention for that person to share the light they have received with the world. One person on fire for Christ can change the world. I truly believe that. In Mark 9:23 Jesus Christ says that anything is possible to anyone that believes. Reaching the world with the gospel of Christ in our generation is possible according to the One who breathed out the stars. If we truly had faith, in the portion of a mustard seed, that God could do what He says, we could turn the world upside down for Christ in this generation. The following is a passage from the Bible where God used a single man to, in the words of others, "turn the world upside down."[1] A vision for the things of God is an essential shift of perspective all of Christ's followers need to see.

VISION OF THE ONE TRUE KING

The phrase “the fear of the Lord” appears 27 times in the Bible. Now, anytime something is mentioned in scripture, it is important and we should pay attention. When something is mentioned more than once in God’s Word, it is of great significance to us. When God inspired those who penned His Words to write a particular phrase 27 times, we would be wise to listen carefully and seek to understand and apply what is being said. The difference between believers whose lives are noticeably changed by God’s Words and those who react with indifference towards them, is that the first group of people are truly saved by God’s grace through faith in Jesus Christ. The second group merely “said a prayer” and “accepted Christ as their personal Savior.” As uncomfortable and unexpected as it may be for you to hear, neither of those phrases are found anywhere at all in scripture. If we are relying on the fact that we said a prayer as our way to Heaven, then the devil has deceived us straight into a Hell that God prepared for him.

Logan started asking me questions about salvation at the age of 4. He was there the night that God broke my heart over my sin that separated me from Him. He saw the change that the gospel had in my life over just a period of a few months. He wanted what I had. To my surprise, one day after talking about Jesus and what He did for us, Logan asked my parents to pray with him as he made a profession of faith in Christ. What Logan failed to do was fully understand the gospel. Logan lived the following years as a good boy that went to church, read his Bible, prayed every day, and everything was good... on the outside.

For years, he inwardly and quietly struggled with his security in Christ. Nobody, including me or any of the rest of his family and friends, would have ever even guessed that he was not a Christian. Now you have to understand that was an openly unashamed Christian who was actually doing things for God including leading others in “the sinner’s prayer.” Deep down he knew something was not right. As he continued to study God’s Word, an uneasiness set as he knew his life was not truly being lived to glorify God, but rather himself. Sure, he knew how to say all the Christian things such as “God first”, “I live for Christ”, and he even occasionally quoted my Instagram name, “Christ is life.” But there was a nearly unexplainable feeling that came over him when he said those things.

Logan dared not tell anyone. I mean, how could he? He had lived a good Christian life, said the right things, stayed out of trouble, hung around the right friends, he even preached several dozen times. Not to mention the souls that he “led to Christ.” People would surely frown upon someone who had done all of this for God without truly being saved himself. He kept brushing off the thought by continually reminding himself that at some point he prayed a prayer. What he was doing, in fact, was choosing to place his reliance on something that he had done Instead of the Son. As I am currently writing this on the first of November, only a few weeks ago, the following story transpired.

It was late in the evening and I had gone to think and pray in a hammock hung between two trees. One tree was strong with its roots grounded deep in the soil and its limbs were sturdy and living. The other tree was weak with parts of its roots were visible on the ground and branches that had fallen off underneath it. After a few minutes, my brother came down and got in another hammock close to mine. My brother and I had long, meaningful talks a number of times and I was always there for him if he ever had questions or needed anything, but he seldom would seek advice or initiate important conversations. This was particularly uncharacteristic of him, so I was beginning to grow curious as to why he came down. After about 30 minutes of rather awkward silence, he finally started telling me about a lot of things the Lord had recently been doing in his heart. Tears began streaming from his eyes like a dripping water faucet. He began to describe how difficult it would be to tell me what he was about to say. As he embarked on the journey of describing what the Lord used in particular to bring him to an understanding that he had never surrendered completely to Jesus as Lord and Savior of his life. I began to cry at the sight of my brother, my best friend since childhood, as he told me of perhaps the most secret thing in his life. He went on to explain that he had never accepted Jesus Christ on His terms. You see, up until this point, Logan loved God a lot. Just not more than himself. He wanted to do what God wanted, but only if God got him what he wanted. Logan claimed to live for God while secretly harboring the real motive behind what he "did for God"-which was to bring attention, popularity, approval, and ultimately glory to himself. My little brother wanted what most Christians want; God and the world at the same time. He wanted to have one foot in the presence of God and one foot holding its place in the world, but at the same time he was desperately striving to get closer to the Father. His efforts were futile. The evil one had deceived him like he has done the majority of those who claim the name of Christ, that he could have the best of both worlds so to speak. That he could enjoy the rich love, joy, peace, and presence of the Father while enjoying the pleasures of sin for a season as well. After all, God would always forgive him right? Wrong. God forgives those of His children that confess their sins to Him and believe that He alone is faithful and just to forgive.[2] What Logan came to realize was that no matter what he did, the reason he could not feel close to the Father was because He did not truly know the Father. He knew plenty about Jesus, but He had never encountered the true Jesus of the Bible. We busted out in worship and admiration to God for bestowing such unconditional love and forgiveness to us through His Son, Jesus Christ. We began praying openly to God like we had never done together before. It was a truly indescribable time that I will never forget. After hours of praying, worshipping, and crying before our Creator, we got up, hugged, and prayed for each other. As incredible as that experience was, it was a tremendous surprise and eye-opener to me. I never thought it was possible for someone who grew up with such over-exposure to the Gospel and to know about Him without truly knowing Him. I came to the realization that there are thousands, if not millions, of proclaimed "Christians" who have never experienced the Christ of scripture.

Logan had a skewed perspective of God. He saw God as Someone who could help him. In his mind, God existed for his gratification. It took a near-death experience of a potentially life-threatening car wreck to strike the fear of the Lord in Logan like never before. But he got it. God does not exist for us. We exist for Him. Our entire purpose of existence on earth is to glorify

God. He does not belong to us. We belong to Him. If we are truly His children, Christ has purchased us with His blood and we are His property. The reason we are here is to glorify and praise The Creator and Savior of our souls. When will we change our perspective from a world-view to a God-view; an eternal view?

Read the following passage of 2 Kings 6:8-17:

> "Then the king of Syria warred against Israel, and took counsel with his servants, saying, In such and such a place shall be my camp. And the man of God sent unto the king of Israel, saying, Beware that thou pass not such a place; for thither the Syrians are come down. And the king of Israel sent to the place which the man of God told him and warned him of, and saved himself there, not once nor twice. Therefore the heart of the king of Syria was sore troubled for this thing; and he called his servants, and said unto them, Will ye not shew me which of us is for the king of Israel? And one of his servants said, None, my lord, O king: but Elisha, the prophet that is in Israel, telleth the king of Israel the words that thou speakest in thy bedchamber. And he said, Go and spy where he is, that I may send and fetch him. And it was told him, saying, Behold, he is in Dothan. Therefore sent he thither horses, and chariots, and a great host: and they came by night, and compassed the city about. And when the servant of the man of God was risen early, and gone

> forth, behold, an host compassed the city both with horses and chariots. And his servant said unto him, Alas, my master! how shall we do? And he answered, Fear not: for they that be with us are more than they that be with them. And Elisha prayed, and said, LORD, I pray thee, open his eyes, that he may see. And the LORD opened the eyes of the young man; and he saw: and, behold, the mountain was full of horses and chariots of fire round about Elisha."

This is an eye-opening story of scripture that explains a transformation of one's perspective on a dramatic scale. In this account in scripture, the king of Syria went to war with Israel. Time after time he secretly planned to defeat Israel, but every time the king of Israel discovered the plans and overcame the Syrian advances. As you could imagine, the king of Syria was enraged as he thought a traitor was amidst one of those he trusted most, and this man was secretly informing Israel of the next move. He angrily asked his men which one of them was on Israel's side. They responded that none of them were, but that a prophet named Elisha was telling the king of Israel the words that the king spoke in his bedroom. The king, most likely confounded and appalled at such news, told his soldiers to go and spy where Elisha was staying so that he could fetch him with the obvious intention of murder. Once they discovered his whereabouts, the king sent what the Bible describes as "a great host" of horses and chariots that came and surrounded the city by night.[3]

In the morning the servant of Elisha arose and saw the immeasurable force that stood around the city. The servant fearfully asked Elisha what they were going to do. The prophet of the Lord told his servant something that most likely made his servant doubt the sanity of Elisha. The prophet told the boy in essence, "Don't be afraid. There are more with us than there are with them."[4] Take a moment and imagine what this young man must have been thinking. "What on earth is this wacko talking about? There are thousands of soldiers with horses and chariots and you are telling me that there is more with us than with them? Where? I do not see anyone else besides us. Perhaps I chose the wrong man of God to pupil." For a few seconds there, he probably thought Elisha was losing his marbles. The servant had a different perspective than the prophet. His eyes were not yet opened to see what Elisha saw.

The servant was so dumbfounded at the sight of the Syrian army in all their awesome wonder that he began to lose hope that he was on the winning side. All he could see was the seemingly hopeless problem. He needed a renewed perspective of his big and powerful God. Elisha, wanting his servant to see, asked the Lord if He would open the young man's eyes. The Lord opened the eyes of the servant and he saw the entire mountain full of horses and chariots of fire all around them. Now put yourself in the boy's shoes and imagine what he must be feeling. The entire Syrian army, that had only moments earlier been the only thing he could see, was now no comparison for the horses and chariots of fire that surrounded them. By opening his eyes, the Lord completely transformed the object to which the servant was looking. God took his eyes off of the problem and onto Himself, the Problem

Solver. Many times we are just as the servant in this passage. We have a limited perspective. We focus on things that God can easily manage. Let us shift our perspectives now so that we can see truth!

As we continue to read, we find that Elisha prays in faith to the Lord a second time asking Him to smite the army with blindness. What God then decides to do is simply incredible. The Bible says, He smites the people with blindness according to the word of Elisha. In other words, the Creator of all Heaven and earth does something that a mere man asks him to do simply because he asked. He grants Elisha this request. Now, keep in mind that Elisha could have asked the Lord to slay every last one of these self-seeking, greed-filled, kill-hungry fools who had come with the purpose of finding, fetching and (according to history) flaying him for their king. The Lord had the power to destroy every last one of these heathen people, but He chose to hearken to the voice of Elisha and smote the entire army with blindness. Imagine what that must have been like. You are standing before thousands of blood-thirsty men who want to end your life when all of the sudden, every one of them goes blind before your presence. That would be pretty jaw-dropping in and of itself.

The Lord then gave Elisha temporary control of the army. This poor army could not get anything right. This is how it is today. God's work is going to be done and He will be glorified in the end. It's ironic that the one job this army had ended up completely backwards to their plan. Instead of capturing Elisha and taking him to their king, the Lord blinded them and they were unknowingly led to the king of Israel by Elisha. Similarly, those who are ruled by the prince of the power of the air, seek to enslave Christ's followers who refuse to remain silent about proclaiming His worthy name. Those who are children of the enemy strive to first overwhelm us. Take a look around you at the modern culture in which we live. There are obvious factors from Hollywood to Disney World that beckon us towards compromising God's standards in order to be more accepting to society. Homosexuals obnoxiously proclaim that they deserve the right to change what God has said is wrong into that which is right in their own eyes. Evolutionist loudly boast that they have the right to believe and impose their beliefs on others by integrating teaching a false theory in public schools and colleges of America. The transgender community argues that they have the right to enter whichever bathroom they feel like entering whether it creates a dangerous atmosphere for others or not. All of these issues stem from the root of pride. Pride is sin and is an abomination to the Lord. The king of sin is the devil. There are, in reality, very few who are bold enough in their beliefs to actually stand out and speak up, but the majority of people either agree with or see nothing wrong with the sin that God hates. All of this is due to our lack of trust in God, which stems from a lost vision of the One true King.

There is an army of unbelievers who have been commissioned by their king to seek, find, discourage, and ultimately destroy any and all who dare to threaten his seemingly overwhelming force. When we see the enemy army, we as children of God have to choices. There are two acronyms for fear. Everyone has a choice to either Forget Everything And Run or Face Everything And Rise. Elisha and his servant chose to face the enemy and rise to the challenge having seen that there are far more with them than there was against them.

How about you? The enemy force that surrounds you may seem overwhelming, but God assures us in His Word that He who lives within us is greater than he who is living in the world.[5] It would quite easy to only focus on that which is seen instead of having faith in that which is unseen-but that would not require faith. God wants to supernaturally break the chains of fear, pride, and addiction that might be holding you back from living a truly abundant life for Him. Will you choose to surrender your will over to His will?

As we continue reading, we will discover the initial reaction of Israel's king when Elisha leads his enemy marching right into the Samaria. Surprisingly, it seems as though the king asks Elisha for permission to destroy them. The king eagerly asks Elisha twice if he can kill the enemy army. Elisha, however, is apparently appalled by such a request. He asked him how he would treat those he captured in battle and then said to treat them the same way. He told the king to give them bread and water and to "make provision for them."[6]

I find it extremely interesting that Elisha responded this way. Personally, if the Lord had just smitten an entire army with blindness, like the king, I would have most likely killed them. I mean, this is your chance, the entire enemy has come stumbling to your gates and they are all severely handicapped. We have to understand that these are more than likely some of the same men that killed many Israelite men. The Israelites were desperately thirsting for revenge and all the sudden, it came knocking on their door. Undoubtedly, what they wanted to do was to kill the entire Syrian army. Nonetheless, the Lord had other plans. The Lord led Elisha to have a forgiving spirit towards his enemies and instead of showing what most would have naturally in the flesh, he was led of the Spirit of God to show kindness and love.

It sure is a good thing he listened to the Lord because it instituted a long period of peace between the nations of Israel and Syria. Similarly, whenever we listen to the Lord by living in active obedience to His will, we will obtain a new perspective and ultimately, peace ourselves. This peace will not be limited to ourselves, but it will overflow into making peace with our enemies. It is not going to be easy. It is not going to be what you feel like doing. However, if the king of Israel would have done what would have been easy and the most reasonable thing, there would have likely been much continuance of fear and strive in generations to come. It is only when we completely surrender our wills to God's will that we discover the peace our souls so desperately desire.

I wholeheartedly believe there is a direct correlation between God's Word and how God wants us to live our daily lives. This historically accurate account was not written to merely fill in space in scripture. God inspired the writer of this book in particular to pen the exact words written for a specific purpose. He wants to teach us something. Are we willing to learn what He has to say? There is a significant difference between learning and listening. Learning requires action and initiates change. Are you willing to change the way you live to model after the example you see in scripture? When we truly do model our lives after scripture and allow God's Word to be the sole influence in our lives then we will see with new eyes. We will see the need of this world as we have never seen before. We will seek to display the gospel of Jesus Christ through every facet of our lives.

I Once was Blind but Now I see

We find yet another biblical account in the gospels where Christ completely altered the sight of a blind man. The following story is inspired by the story of Jesus healing the blind man in John 9 and is written with elaboration to enhance your imagination. In preparation to reading this section, get a copy of God's Word and read John 9.

"Congratulations, I'm so happy for you!" said the friends and family of the newlyweds. "I hope it is a boy" exclaimed the father. "I am praying for a girl" proclaimed the mother. Their baby was due any day now, and they were ecstatic to say the least! The upcoming dad had already build a bed and the soon to be mom had already started decorating the room. Excited energy filled the air of their home and radiated from the both of them.

Finally, the day they had been anxiously awaiting arrived. It was a precious, healthy boy. In the beholding eyes of the parents they had a perfect, beautiful, baby boy. He was flawless and their love for him was beyond words. He slowly grew and as he got older, they noticed that something was not quite right. When they played peek-a-boo with him at a few weeks, he would not respond. He would not giggle like the other babies. It did not take long for the loving parents to discover that their cherished child was blind.

The boy soon grew into a man and eventually became a beggar. Life was difficult. He barely scraped by from day to day on the alms that people who gave to him out of pity. One day Jesus Christ passed by him. Jesus had so much love and compassion that He could not leave the man in his helpless state. Jesus spat on the ground and made clay to anoint the eyes of the blind man. The Messiah then proceeded to tell him to go and wash in the pool of Siloam. The blind man did exactly as Jesus commanded him and soon after this blind man returned seeing. Jesus Christ did something that had never been done since the world began; He opened the eyes of one born blind.

Jesus says the man was born blind so "that the works of God should be manifest in him."[7] Likewise, you and I have been born blind. Once you are saved by grace through faith in Christ alone He has "called you out of darkness into His marvelous light."[8] Since we have been transformed from blind to seeing, we should be Christ's ambassadors boldly sharing the light we have received with a world who is in desperate need.

You see, in the beginning, God created us perfect before Him. We were spotless, blameless, and sinless. God had fellowship with us. The Creator of all physically walked with His creation who willingly chose to abide by His laws so we could experience closeness with Him. It was, in the words of God, "good." There was no sin. There was no pain. There was no disease. There was no confusion. There was no depression. There was no suffering. There was no destruction. There was no temptation. There was no death. God created and it was *very good.*[9]

Creation was so good, but it did not last. Humanity chose to rebel and sin against a holy God. The payment for sin was eternal separation from God in an awful place called Hell. However, because God is loving and merciful, He provided a way for us to get back to perfect fellowship with Him through faith in His Son, Jesus Christ. Now that we know that Christ died and rose again to pay for sin and to conquer the power of sin and death, we begin to see with new eyes. This vision is unlike anything the world has to offer. This new perspective is essential to the Christian life.

Challenge

Perspective is key. The lens that you view life through changes everything. What is your perspective on life? Have you asked the Lord to open your eyes so that you can see what He sees? God's vision is a world vision. Do you share God's vision for all to come to repentance and trust in Christ alone for salvation? When you get outside of your comfort zone and obey Christ's commands, you will discover that the only vision worth having is God's vision and you will ask Him to reveal His vision for the world to you.

Chapter 4

Problems: When Things Do Not Go as You Originally Planned

My friend Andre has an interesting story about when things do to not as planned. Andre grew up in a broken home. He has never met or seen his earthly father. His mother had him when she was a teenager and gave him to his grandmother to raise. He never heard the words "I love you." He did not know love and as a result, he never learned how to show love and receive love from others. When Andre was in the 6th grade, he moved to my city. He had no idea that this move would set him up to encounter the source of all love, Jesus Christ.

When I first met Andre, he was living for the world. Andre was still young and had no interest in anyone or anything other than himself. He lived for the sole purpose of bringing fleeting pleasure to himself. He was disrespectful to his teachers in order to look cool and be accepted by his peers. He lived to glorify his own name. Yet, this attitude and mentality put him into the position to discover his emptiness. Andre knew that there had to be more to life and he was seeking something more that would not leave him feeling so empty inside. What he was about to discover was that the something he longed for was actually a Someone who could provide the everlasting satisfaction his soul desperately desired! Jesus Christ radically transformed every aspect of his life.

Andre is a real person with a real story and his testimony is one of redemption. The Lord saw fit to use me to introduce him to the Savior! He now wakes up early every morning to spend quality time in God's Word. He has a genuine relationship with the Heavenly Father! He is growing in Christ! He is becoming an effective witness for the Savior! I have witnessed first-hand that Jesus still saves!

Jesus is the same yesterday, today, and forever.[1] He never changes. Although society, culture, and countries may change, Jesus Christ and His Word endures forever.

If every follower of Christ lived in relentless surrender to God's will, this world would be undoubtedly changed. But somewhere along the way we have ceased to believe that God can use us to accomplish His will in us. We have let our natural born, deceitfully wicked hearts talk us into remaining complacent in our walk with Christ.

Complacency is one of the greatest enemies to the cross of Christ, and it is a problem every follower of Christ will face. Complacency is when one has uncritical self-satisfaction in his or her own achievements. This is putting ourselves above the work of Christ. When we decide that our work for Christ is good enough and we think that we have done enough our spiritual life crumbles. Not only for us, but for those around us. One thing that has been made abundantly clear to me in my brief time on earth is that complacency is very contagious. It is like a spark in an oil field. When Christ's followers become complacent in their relationship with Him, their relationship with others will also grow complacent. Determine never to get to a place of complacency in your walk with the Lord.

Another deadly disease that plagues Christianity as a whole is apathy. Apathy is the lack of passion, emotion, or excitement. Many Christians have fallen into an apathetic state of mind. I have been apathetic towards the things of God before and I am sure that you have been as well. Apathy can destroy a church and the motivation of Christ's followers to reach the world for Jesus Christ. Apathy will steal your desire to know Christ and share Him with a world that is in desperate need. Apathy is dangerous because when we are nonchalant about Jesus and what He has done for us, we will not be actively sharing Him with others. Those who we fail to share God's Word with will spend an eternity in a real place called Hell. Therefore, it is vitally important that we are constantly seeking God's Word and striving to live in obedience to Christ's commands as a result of our love for Him.

Guard your heart against both complacency and apathy. Both of these attributes are extremely detrimental to the Christian life. One cannot be on fire for God with these two feelings living inside his or her heart. Always keep Christ at the forefront of all so that you are less prone to slip into these ideals that directly contradict God's plan and the display of His love through us.

I cannot imagine how one could claim to have the Creator of love living inside them and harbor so much hatred towards those He created and loves deeply. It is an oxymoron. An illustration of how that might look would be a husband saying that he loves his wife by telling her once a day, but never talks to her at all after that. He does not contribute financially in the least, but rather sits on the couch all day and either plays video games or watches TV. The only time he gets up is to get food and drink. When his wife comes home from working all day, he expresses no gratitude. He expects her to wait on him and serve him until he is perfectly satisfied. On the occasion that she refuses or sits down to rest, he becomes angry and starts yelling at her. The actions of the man do not reflect the love that he proclaimed. He is a hypocrite. He justifies his actions by the simple fact that he told his wife he loves her.

Many of those who claim to be Christians act in a similar way. If we are being completely honest with ourselves, many times, we express to the Lord and others that we love God, yet our actions reflect otherwise. You see, it is impossible to love God and not love those whom He loves. Actions speak louder than words. God loves people. Not just us, but everyone. He desires that none should perish in Hell, but that all should come to repentance. He chooses to use us to relay that message to others. Are you willing to be used?

Putting God in His Rightful Place

When God is first in our lives, He replaces our worries and doubts with faith and trust in Him. It is amazing that when we take a step of faith by deciding that God is able to do great things in and through us, awesome things happen! In our minds we often attempt to put God in a box. We take Him out and show Him off like He is ours to control and use as we please. For a few hours a week at church we let Him out and let Him rule our lives. And then, after only a few short hours, we return to "normal life." We put Him right back in the box we have created and forget about Him.

How disgusted the Creator must be with the way that His creation often treats Him. Too many times we forget that the King of the world is not ours to use as we please. He does not belong to us. He is not our pet. He is the Almighty God of untold galaxies. He is not in our hands, we are in His hands.[2] We cannot fit the infinite, untamable God into a box.

Our perspective of the Almighty is flawed. Yes, we pray to Him, but the majority of the time our prayers are centered towards ourselves. Dear God, please bless me. Dear God, please heal me. Dear God, please fix all of these problems in my life. Many times we only go to God either out of a lifeless habit or because we want something from Him. Because of this, we are missing the entire blessing of prayer. The fact that we, who were once enemies of the Lord, can freely talk to Him is an honor that we take for granted.

When did we forget that God is the King of the world? He owns everything. He is omnipotent. He alone is sovereign. He hangs the world on nothing. Almighty God is the sole orchestrator and operator of all creation. He has always been and will always be. The wonderful thing is that, in Christ, we have access to all that He is! You see, once Christ is our life, God's Word says that we belong to Him. He will one day be Savior and Lord of all, and we must determine to make Him Savior and Lord of our lives now.

God is Not a Dog

"How dare you even make such an assumption!" responded friends when I mentioned how they habitually treated God. "The Almighty should never be compared to a dog!" they exclaimed. While I agree that it is perhaps an extreme example, I am afraid that it is a fitting way to illustrate how we often treat the Creator. Whether we like to admit it or not, the way many people (including myself in the past) treat God as if He belongs to us. It is almost as if He is someone that we have in our possession instead of the One that holds us.

During my childhood, my family always owned dogs. Dogs love to play. Dogs love to cuddle up right up next to you and let you rub their bellies. Dogs live for you to give them attention. There is one thing that I have noticed every dog has in common. All dogs love to eat. They always seem hungry. When it is getting cold outside, even when they are stuffed full of food, they will continue to eat more in preparation for the coming winter. Although I have always thought it sounded silly, the saying is true that at times, a dog can seem like a man's best friend. My dog Piper, for example, has been there for me through a lot. She never seems to change in her affection for me. When others yell at me and let me down, she still walks over to me and seems happy to see and spend time with me. When I went through my first break up, Piper was there to comfort me and cheer me up. In the same way that my dog seemed unchanging, faithful, and loving, God seems to be similar in those specific aspects.

Think about it. The purpose of a dog's existence is to bring gratification to its master. A dog lives to please his master. Is that not how we, many times, treat God? Often times, it is easy to get into the groove of treating God as if He exists solely for us. We only go to him when we need Him, or we think He needs us. By constantly giving Him our words and scarcely receiving and obeying His words, we are feeding Him and starving ourselves. Our problem is that we often treat God in this same manner. I have a bit of shocking news for you. God does not need us. The Creator has existed for an eternity past without us and will continue to live whether or not we choose Him. He does not need us to "feed Him" with our words while all but ignoring His Word. He does not need us to "play with Him" as if He were a pet that needed exercise. He does not need us to give Him attention or affection like an animal. In fact, unlike many think, God does not actually need us at all.

God wants us. He created us because He is love and He loves us. Out of all created species, we are the chosen recipients of God's love. He wants to use us. He wants to bestow upon us the richest of blessings, but we must first stop treating Him like He is ours to do with what we want, tell Him what we want Him to do, and expect the One who spoke the world into existence to obey us whom He created. He is the Creator. He speaks and we are to obey. Not the other way around. He will do what He wants to do with or without our help. He does not need us. He wants us. Do we want Him? Do our actions reflect that we truly love Him more than we love ourselves?

Why God Gives Us Guidelines

The reason God gives us guidelines is not because He wants to boss us around and make us miserable, but out of His infinite love for us. They are not rules that He gives us because He hates us, but a guide that we can follow to experience further peace, joy, and love than we could never know otherwise. Do not look at the guidelines God gives us in His Word as an impenetrable wall; look at them instead as the lines in the middle of the road that separate the lanes. If your boss gives you rules and you break them, the consequences of those choices would be termination from that job. On a road, however, you have the freedom to pass over on the other side, but the consequences of your decisions would be exceedingly dangerous and potentially disastrous.

God gives us guidelines because He loves us. I grew up with a "do this" and "do not do that" mentality. People were always telling me that I should behave a certain way, but never gave me any biblical enforced reasons why. They told me I should go to church every Sunday, read my Bible every day, and pray multiple times a day. I did. I found myself in a meaningless routine of going through the motions. I felt lukewarm and was sick at the thought of making God unhappy. I later realized that what I was doing was no different than mere religion. I felt just as empty and unsatisfied as unsaved individuals I knew. My problem was believing and following people more than God. This problem was solved by personal study of God's Word.

When I stopped doing what people said because they told me to and started doing what God says in His Word, I discovered a renewed purpose and joy in life. I realized that God desires to show us His power. He desires that we fall in love with Him. He wants us to experience joy that we can only find when we obey His Word by applying it to our lives.

People often ask me "how can I apply God's Word to my life?" I respond by telling them to go home and read a certain passage as intently as they would a love letter written by someone they loved. I then tell them to fervently ask the Lord in prayer to reveal what He wants to teach them and how they can apply what He says to their life. I find that most of the time people do not care enough to even bother trying, but the few people who are serious about serving God with their lives find that God's will is clearly revealed in God's Word.

God commands us to do things because he known we will find infinitely more joy and satisfaction in Him than in our feeble attempts to find joy and satisfaction in anything that the world has to offer. We can only find true and real satisfaction in God. For instance, He does not command in Mark 16:15 that we go into all the world and preach the gospel to every creature because He wants us to experience rejection, suffering, and persecution. He commands us to go into all the world because He knows that in the midst of trials, He will build patience in us and we will be made stronger and more content with Him alone. He wants to give us the peace, joy, and satisfaction of being used to lead others to Christ! He wants to use us to bring others to Him.

Although we will find peace by living in obedience to the Bible, it is not God's primary purpose that we do things for His Kingdom, but that we become one who is totally surrendered to His will above our own. It is far more important to the King that we become who we are in Him than it is that we do things for Him. The Father enjoys quality amount of time spent with Him far more than He does quantity amount of time doing things for Him. The honest fact is that there is absolutely nothing that we could ever do to make God love us less than He does at this moment and there is nothing we could ever do to make Him love us more than He already does. We are unconditionally loved by Love Himself. What a mystery that we, who were once enemies of God, could be reconciled to Him through Jesus Christ! This love the real reason for guidelines. God loves us so much that He will give us the knowledge through His word to do what is right and live for Him. These are why God gives us guidelines, for our betterment and so that we have a greater structure of priorities in our lives.

Challenge

The problems that have happened in your life will either make you or break you. How you respond to difficult circumstances you face will determine how effective you will allow Christ to use you. No matter what, God will be glorified in us. How we choose to give Him glory is a decision that is up to us. If you truly want to make Christ your life, you will surrender and walk in obedience to His will in the midst of your problems. Always keep in mind that God loves you and only wants the best for you. The end result of God allowing things to happen to His children is for our good and His glory.

Chapter 5

Patience: Actively Waiting on God's Perfect Timing

Patience is a virtue that does not come with birth. Patience is not easy to obtain. Although we are not naturally patient and it often takes months of hardships, trials, and difficulties to teach us, Patience is worth it.

In a study conducted by a researcher, every student of a particular preschool class received a single marshmallow. They were told that if they could resist the overwhelming urge to eat the marshmallow for five minutes, they would receive a second marshmallow. Further follow-up analyzations show that those who exemplified enough patience to win the second fluffy sugar-filled treat, accomplished exponentially superior potential success in the rest of their lives. They were more likely than the impetuous children to earn higher salaries and less likely to become dependent on all types of addictions. As a result of the research, we can conclude that those who choose to defer immediate gratification by exercising patience, experienced much greater success in life.

For the large majority of people, patience does not come naturally. When we do go through periods of patience, it's often temporary. Most of the time, we go too fast, we are tempted to lose our cool when people squeeze ahead of us in line, we are eager to interrupt in conversations, we prefer to buy now and pay later because it's easier- because it is what *we want* to do. We often regret things we say and wish they had never been said. Additionally we also make decisions in haste that cause a tremendous amount of future pain, fear, and regret. I can remember one instance in particular where I acted impetuously and paid (quite literally) for it.

I was working at an arcade and finally got off at two in the morning. Andre, Logan, and I had worked a twelve-hour day and were completely exhausted. We stumbled to the car and both of my companions started drifting off to sleep. I was struggling to stay awake like a five-year-old in church when there is a monotone preacher speaking. I was fighting with all I had in me to stay awake long enough to get home. After a few tortuous moments of driving, I saw the blinding blue and red lights flashing behind me. In shock, I instantly pulled over and began breathing heavy as if I had suddenly been awakened from a deep sleep. Logan and Andre immediately woke up and began grumbling and yelling at me, when I was honestly wondering what I did wrong. As I rolled down the window the officer shined his flashlight in my eyes and uttered those infamous words, "Sir, do you know why I pulled you over?" From a half asleep, half frightened voice, I exclaimed, "I'm sorry, but no sir, I do not." He then responded by telling me that I was going sixty in a thirty-five, and was accelerating higher. As if that was not enough, he also said that my headlights were off. Now, in my defense, there are bright street lights all along the road and the speed limit signs are no bigger than twelve-inch ruler; not to mention the fact that it was two in the morning and I was not the most alert individual after working twelve hours straight. Nevertheless, I did not explain those things to him, but simply apologized. He asked what we were doing up there so late and I was so fatigued that I told him "Taglazer" instead of Lazertag. After that (I genuinely thought he was about to ask me to step out of the vehicle and walk in a straight line) he asked to see my license and registration. Praise the Lord that I had my license on me, but the registration for the van was nowhere to be found.

After several agonizing minutes that seemed like hours, the officer returned and told me that the total ticket should cost me around four-hundred dollars. The blood instantly drained from my face as I imagined how I would explain all of this to my parents. Thankfully, by God's grace, the officer let me off with a small citation of only a portion of the cost. I was beyond grateful for the grace of the Father and learned a very important lesson that night- slow down. There is something calming about those words, slow down. It seems that there is a certain indescribable peace about slowing down. We live in a society that screams "Go as fast as you can," "Time is money. So don't ever take a break," "Get as much as you can in the smallest amount of time possible," "If you slow down, even just a bit, you will be run over." From online banking to fast food restaurants, the culture around us constantly encourages and enables us to get things done in the fastest way possible no matter the cost. But you may be wondering, "What is the cost?" I mean, let's be realistic for a second. What is the harm in going fast? Inventors are coming up with new inventions every day that seek to make our lives better by saving us more time so that we can continue to speed by on the highway of life. Entrepreneurs stake their entire livelihoods on creating better products and services that will be able to enhance our lives so that we can be more effective with our time and money. But does this truly make us happy? Does going faster to make more money to buy more things that will one day be replaced by other things that will ultimately be burned, *really* bring us satisfaction? No.

Patience is something nearly unheard of in our present society. Self-control and patience go hand in hand with one another. Just a few days ago, (as I am writing this book) less than fifteen minutes away from our house, two men were driving in two separate vehicles at a gas station parking lot. When one of them was about to back into another car, the other honked to let him know about the possible collision. Witnesses say that after some verbal altercation between the two, one man became irritated because the driver in front of him was going too slowly. This man got out of his car, pulled out a gun from his pocket, shot the man 7 consecutive times in the chest, and walked back to his car. I suppose after sitting in his car a few minutes and realizing the consequences of his actions, this man decided to take his own life. The authorities found no past criminal record of the shooter. Deputies said the two men did not know each other. This is an extreme case of impatience and a lack of self-control that shocked thousands in my city.

An Impatient Generation

We live in a generation that wants what they want, when they want it, and the exact way they want it. Asking us to wait patiently for God to supply every one of our needs is just as likely as giving a scrawny dog a rack of baby-back ribs and asking him to save it for tomorrow. We are accustomed to getting everything we want, and quite frankly, we do not want to wait. We often impatiently cry out "Why?!" when we do not understand the answers to various questions that come our way. We do not want to cook because that takes too long, so we frequent the microwave more often than the oven: then become frustrated when we have to get up and go get our zapped food after the annoying radioactive-consumed box beeped ten consecutive times. We repeatedly tap our foot in an eager haste to get our food at the fast-food drive through. We are quick to become enraged when we are cut off by the driver next to us. We audaciously object to anyone telling us the truth as it temporarily wounds our pride.

In the Bible, we see multiple examples of the Lord building patience in people's lives. It is often easy to look at people in the Bible as superheroes. We think that because certain people made it to the esteemed *Hall of Faith,* that they are somehow superior or supernatural. They are not. They are just people like you and I. The difference between them and us is the amount of faith they exemplified. Take the story of Abraham and Sarah for example. Abraham was no extraordinary individual. He was a man that simply believed God and was willing to patiently wait on Him.

In the following paragraphs I am going to give you a brief summary of Abraham's life with the focus on the patience that God built in Him. In preparation to this portion, I would like you to stop reading for a second. That's right, put down this book and go get a Bible. Please follow along in scripture and study along with me the story of one of the most mightily used men in all of the Bible. In Genesis 12:1, we see that God tells Abraham to get out of his country, leave his family and his father's house, and go to a place that God would show him. Wow. Take a moment with me and imagine if God gave us that same command today. How would you respond if the Creator of all spoke to you and told you to leave where you are and go somewhere that he would reveal to you while you obediently followed His command? You may be thinking, "That's insane! There is no way I could have *that much* faith!" But deep down inside, you wish you could have enough faith in the One who spoke the world into existence that you could obediently do what He says. I mean, although that would be totally crazy, He is capable of providing for us and protecting us if we are living in obedience to Him, right?

Mind Blown

"I am about to blow your mind" was a phrase that I heard many times growing up. Most of the time it was in math class by a teacher who loved to blow students minds with some ungodly exponential equation. There is a certain unexplainable wonder of our awareness over a proclaimed truth that can be described in no other way than "mind blown." You ready to have your mind blown? Well, ready or not, here it comes- The exact same God that called Abraham to leave all that he had and knew, is calling us to abandon our ambitions, goals, dreams, and entire lives all for Him. That's right, Jesus Christ has commanded His followers to go into all the world and preach His gospel to every creature.[1]

The Mysterious Call

I tell people that the last command Christ has given us ought to be our first priority, I find the responses I hear shockingly surprising. It is especially peculiar to me how so many proclaimed Christians find intricate ways to reword or add words to that verse of scripture. I have heard countless times that this verse only applies to those who have received a loud, dramatically miraculous voice from God Himself. Most Christians that I have talked to about this, say that those who have not heard this esoteric voice are automatically exempt from Christ's command to go. Somehow, millions of proclaimed Christians translate this verse into "Stay ye therefore in your own country and listen to preaching of the gospel." This is no less than the complete opposite of Christ's original command.

"Why," Christians ask "are there still those who have never once heard the gospel? Has God not called more missionaries into the world to reach the heathen with Christ?" The answer I frequently tell them is, "Yes," God has called more to get involved in global evangelism, but few are willing to answer the call. Millions around the world are walking blindfolded into a Christ-less eternity because we, unlike Abraham, have refused to answer the call.

How about you? If you claim to be a follower of Christ, He has called *you* to "go into all the world and preach the gospel to every creature."[2] So you must make a decision to either do what Christ wants by "going and teaching" or do what you want by "staying and receiving." You will never hear a mysterious voice from Heaven telling you in a deep voice to "Go." Jesus has already commanded and called you to do what He wants. How you respond to His call is your choice entirely. But let me just tell you that if Abraham had done what *he wanted,* what was *easier and more comfortable,* He would have never received blessing from the Lord. He would have never become "The father of many nations."[3] If you truly want to be used of the Lord, He will use you to accomplish things infinitely superior to your wildest imagination. If however, you do not want to be used by God, He will use another. You see, God does not need you, He wants you. He has already called you. Will you answer His call?

Excuses

As we continue studying through the story of Abraham, we see that after The Lord promises to bless Abraham and cause him to be a blessing to every family of the earth, Abraham departed. He took his wife Sarah, his nephew Lot, all the possessions he had acquired throughout his life, and all of his servants into the land of Canaan. Oh, and by the way, I nearly forgot to mention that Abraham was seventy-five years old when he obeyed the Lord by answering his call. The fact that God called and used a man who was elderly gives no elderly aged people the excuse that they are too old for God to use them. Likewise, if God can use one who has exceeded the years of their prime, to accomplish big things for God, it obviously proves that He is more than capable and willing to use those who are under the age of seventy-five. Therefore, age is not a factor when it comes to answering God's call. There is not a single excuse worth the value of rejecting the call of God. We need to automatically eliminate all excuses and obediently follow God's call.

Notice that Abraham refrained from using any excuses and simply obeyed God. This should be an example to us all of how to respond to the Lord's commands. As Abraham and his family ventured out on this unique nomadic journey, they came into the glorious city of Canaan. There the Lord promised to give that land unto his seed (that he did not even have at the time). Abraham, in return built an altar to the Lord. At the end of verse seven, we find a small phrase that ought to automatically grab our attention "And there builded he an altar to unto the Lord, who appeared unto him."[34] I believe that it is important to recognize the fact that the Lord met with the patriarch only after Abraham stopped what he was doing, obeyed His command without hesitation, and believed God's promises enough to build an altar unto Him. By default we, as God's children, can conclude that only if we repent from sin, obey the Lord's command without hesitation, and believe that God is capable of fulfilling the promises that He has given us, will The Lord meet with us.

FEAR

As Abraham continues his journey a fierce famine struck the land. Food was very scarce in the land of Canaan. Egypt however, seemed to have enough food during this "*grievous*" time of hunger. So, Abraham decided to temporarily stay there until the famine was over. In verses eleven through thirteen, we see the first mentioned compromise of Abraham's faith in the Lord. What was his downfall? Fear. Fear is merely another twisted form of pride as it demonstrates a lack of trust in God and causes us to think about our own well-being. Consider the previous statement for a moment.

Whenever we are afraid it is because we do not want to fail. Whether we are afraid of failing ourselves, others, or God, every time fear is present in our lives pride is also present. God hates pride. We will discuss pride in detail at a later chapter, but it is necessary to note that Abraham was thinking about only himself when he requested that his wife, Sarah, pose as his sister. Although this was a half-truth in the eyes of people, it was a whole-lie in the eyes of God. As we will see in the following sentences, Abraham's seemingly insignificant happy medium approach to attempting to solve a problem on his own nearly lead to the defilement of God's vessel that He was to use to fulfill His plan for the coming Messiah. Not only that, but because Abraham was afraid for his life (that God had already promised to bless every nation of the world out of) Pharaoh and the entirety of his house were plagued.

Just like Abraham anticipated, when he came into Egypt the Egyptians looked at Sarah and were stunned by her beauty. Pharaoh's princes were so amazed that that scripture says they "*commended*' her before the king.[5] I can imagine what they said to Pharaoh to be something similar to what I have repeatedly heard guys tell me when they see a beautiful girl. "Bro, this is the hottest girl on the entire planet! You have got to meet her! If you are too afraid to talk to her, I will hook you up with her digits." While I am sure that is not the exact lingo they used to commend her to Pharaoh, it certainly seems like it must have been along those lines in my imagination. Anyways, when they told the most powerful man of the known world at the time, you can assume what happened next. That's right, Pharaoh took her into his house. Now, it was not like he just stole her for nothing in return. He blessed Abraham abundantly. The Bible says in verse sixteen, that '*he entreated Abraham well for her sake*".[6] He gave him sheep, oxen, donkeys, servants, and camels.

I believe it is important for us to note that when we sin, the world richly rewards us. It is also vital to remember that the world's "*pleasures*" only last *"for a season"*.[7] Had Abraham trusted God completely, He might not have gotten presents from the world, but He would surely have received far greater gifts from the Giver of all good things.[8]

As we continue to read in verse 17, it is evident that God plagued Pharaoh and his house with what the Bible describes as "*great plagues*" all because of Sarah's sake.[9] Pharaoh was furious that he had been lied to. I find it surprising and interesting that as quickly as Pharaoh was willing to give them livestock and servants, he was eager to send them away. I think this is a perfect illustration that God gives us concerning the way the world treats us. The world and its pleasures are always temporary. There is a phrase that I have heard many times that exemplifies this truth- Sin will take you farther than you ever wanted to go, keep you longer than you ever wanted to stay, and cost you far more than you ever wanted to pay. This world promises much, but fulfills little. God, however is trustworthy. He has never once failed and never will. His rewards, although they come at a price of complete trust in Him, are eternally more rewarding than any sin.

What can we learn from this? Small compromises always lead to potentially disastrous consequences. I believe that you and I can learn many valuable truths from this one passage of scripture about patience. Although God blessed Abraham in the midst of his rebellion to Him, He wanted to bless him in far greater ways. Faith in God includes faith in His timing. When you and I are willing to deny the urge to rush into what we think we want, and simply wait patiently on His perfect timing, He will bless us far beyond our wildest imagination!

When Helping Actually Hurts

One day in an enchanting forest deep in the heart of the Appalachian Mountains, a boy named Jacob was on an adventurous journey to locate and help as many creatures as possible. As he was stumbling through the woods, he discovered a fascinating caterpillar. He gently picked it up and excitedly took it home to show his mother. When she told him he could keep it if he took good care of it, he was filled with happiness! The boy retrieved a jar from a drawer and began to put a variety of plants for it to eat and a stick for it to climb on in the jar. Every day he watched the caterpillar grow and continued to bring it new plants to eat.

One day, the caterpillar climbed near the top of the stick and started behaving abnormally. It began to vibrate and quiver while coiling some type of silk around itself. The boy worriedly called his mother into the room who knew that the caterpillar was weaving a cocoon. The mother began to explain to the boy that the caterpillar was going through a metamorphosis where it was becoming a butterfly. The boy was thrilled to hear about the changes his caterpillar would go through. He intently the cocoon daily in anxious anticipation for the butterfly to emerge. One day, the cocoon began shaking back and forth until, suddenly, a small hole appeared in the silky-shell. The boy could see that the caterpillar who had gone into the cocoon was no longer the same creature that was struggling endlessly to come out.

When the boy first saw it trying to come out, he was initially excited. However, he slowly became concerned when he saw this mysterious new creation frantically beating its wings against the protective covering trying to get free. The butterfly was struggling so hard to get out! It seemed so desperate! It appeared to be making no progress! The boy could not resist the overwhelming desire to intervene. He hastily ran to get some scissors and snipped the cocoon to make a larger hole and the butterfly quickly emerged! As the butterfly came out, the boy was surprised. It had a swollen body, and tiny, shriveled wings. He carefully continued watching the butterfly expecting its wings would begin to dry out, enlarge, and expand to support the swollen body.

He was certain that, in time, the body would get smaller and the wings would grow to sustain the body when in suspended in the air. But neither happened! The butterfly spent all of the days of its life crawling around with an obese body and miniature wings. It was never able to fly...

As the boy was pondering what had gone wrong, his mother took him to talk to a nature specialist. The specialist explained that when the butterfly comes out of its cocoon, the only way to strengthen its wings is by beating them against the cocoon. The boy learned that the butterfly was *supposed to* struggle. The butterfly's struggle to push its way through the tiny opening of the protective casing actually pushes the fluid out of its body and into the wings so it can fly. Without the struggle of trying to get out, the butterfly would never have the ability to get off the ground in flight. Although the boy had good intentions of helping the butterfly, he actually disabled it from fulfilling its purpose.

You and I can learn many lessons from this story. However, we are going to zone in on the fact that if the boy could only have had enough patience to let the butterfly develop its wings on its own in its own time, then the butterfly could have had a much more enjoyable life. In a similar way, God works on a different time table than we do, and we must be willing to patiently wait on His perfect timing until we reach our full potential in Him. Many times this includes struggle. It will not be easy, but then again, does anything that is truly worth having come easy? I am convinced that all good things come to those who wait. Nothing lasting and beautiful is easily obtained. Love is no exception.

Love is Patient

The Bible says that it is evident that love requires patience. "Charity suffereth long, and is kind; charity envieth not; charity vaunteth not itself, is not puffed up" In my very limited time on this earth, I have found that without patience, love is merely a word.[10] In order for true love to exist there must be action. Love is an action verb. Action is the determining factor that distinguishes true love from a fleeting feeling often referred to as lust.

Love and lust, although many believe that these two concepts are the same, the opposite is true. Love and lust are exceptionally different in every way. Lust envies. Love endures. Lust is temporary. Love is lasting. Lust is brief. Love is eternal. Lust is a feeling. Love is an action. Sometimes it does not feel like love is an action, but I assure you it is. Patience can seem as merely waiting, the absence of not really doing anything, yet the truth is that true patience is real work. Look at it this way- To have patience is to actively live in obedience to God's commands while trusting Him to direct each step you take in the future. As you are actively wait on the Lord by doing what you already know He wants you to do, He will place the right people and circumstances into your life in His perfect timing with the intention of bringing you closer to Him.

The following words are difficult for me to write about, but they illustrate a significant example of how the Lord taught me patience in a premature dating relationship. I was recently in a dating relationship with a wonderful, Godly girl. She was in love with Jesus and was actively involved in getting His gospel to the world. She was not the ordinary stereotypical girl who only did things for herself; she was unselfishly seeking the Lord for every aspect of her life. There was something about her that automatically grabbed my attention and peaked my interest to want to learn more about her. The Lord truly directed the beginning of our friendship and we acted as if we had been friends our entire lives. We had much in common and were passionate about the same things- Knowing God and making Him known to the world! We were "just friends" for several months. We would talk frequently and before long, our friendship gradually began transform into something more than a friendship. Due to previous friendships with girls who were not content to be "just friends," I took (what I thought to be) a slow and cautious approach to "the next step" in our relationship. I liked being "just friends." It simply felt more comfortable and less awkward. Nevertheless, there was a certain unexplainable desire to be more than friends. We had a long distance friendship. I would come to the state she was living in to preach and for special events at a few churches where I could see her. One time she even drove up to my city to spend time with my family and me! All of this was incredible, exciting, and... perfect. Over time, whether it was the pressure from friends and family, or the exciting mysteriousness of trying something new, I decided to tell her that I loved her and hoped to date her with the intent of marriage in the future. For the first time in my entire life, I actually attempted to be romantic. I had picked a delicately beautiful rose off a rosebush outside my house and had previously bought her a necklace. She excitedly told me she would love to, but that I would have to ask her dad first. This seemed to be inevitable. I distinctly remember coming to visit her home to talk to her dad after a summer missions camp. Living in a different state and all, I was not the closest with their family and, as a result, it was a bit awkward (as you could imagine). I was inside helping her pack some things for her missions trip the following week when her dad asked me to follow him outside so we could talk. He held a pistol in his hand. I gulped and sheepishly followed the man with the gun outside. To my utter amazement, he proceeded to load and cock the firearm while looking directly in my eyes, and inquired if there was something I wanted to ask him. I was momentarily caught off guard. The entire two-hour drive down I was practicing what I was going to say, but at that exact moment, with a loaded gun in front of me, I completely forgot everything that I had prepared. My mind was racing, but it felt as if my tongue was being held at gunpoint. I felt as if I was an actor on stage in front of a large audience with every esteemed person I knew in attendance; I had only one line and I had forgotten it. In a rush back to reality, I uttered these exact words: "Would it be alright if I started talking to your daughter?" I felt like a complete idiot. My face instantly became as red as a ripe tomato in humiliation. "Wow" I thought, "I just completely butchered that opportunity." Thankfully, he inferred from that awful way of putting it, that I meant dating, and he helped me out by saying, "If you are asking if I am alright with you dating my daughter, you have my full consent." He added. "On one condition- that you love her the same way that Christ loves the church." I emphatically agreed although I was honestly shocked at his response. I mean, I knew that I truly loved his daughter and only had her best interest in mind, but I only had the opportunity to speak with him once or twice before this moment. How did he know who I was and trust me with his daughter? I later learned that he trusted me because I had a good reputation and was reminded of the truth of God's Word when Solomon says a good name is rather to be chosen than great riches![11]

Anyhow, after I got that off my chest, I was relieved to hear that we were invited to a friend's birthday party. As she got into my car, a strange feeling came over us now that we had "officially crossed the line" of friendship to romantic relationship. This never felt very natural. It was not sinful or wrong, but it was just different. It was a wonderful day that we were able to spend together and we had a good time. In the days and weeks ahead, all seemed to be going great. Life was full of happiness. We would share with each other what we learned each day from the Bible and talk often about taking Christ's gospel to the nations.

I felt like I was living in a dream. I had everything I wanted and needed. I truly thought we were going to date until we got married. I mean, why else would God send this beautiful amazing girl into my life? I was sure that she was the one for me and that I was in the center of God's will by dating her. However, as you are about to discover, she obviously did not reflect my same feelings.

We set aside time daily to talk to each other. We would call and talk about how God was working in our lives at the end of each day. One night, she asked me to call her. My girlfriend decided that we should break up. That night the Lord broke me. I learned about more patience in a few moments than what many people learn in a lifetime. Looking back now, I see how good God is and the blessing disguised in this breakup. Nevertheless, at the time, I was genuinely heartbroken. I tried to go on with life as if nothing happened, but it was apparent that I was struggling. For several weeks, the Lord kept breaking me down until He had me exactly where he wanted me- broken, on my knees, and forced to rely solely on and wait patiently upon Him alone. The Lord is continuing to build patience in me and I have by no means "arrived" spiritually. I readily admit that have much more to learn and am excited about how God is going to continue to teach me patience. By God's grace, I can say with full confidence that I have no regrets and I am truly content with Christ alone! Jesus is sufficient for me. He has never failed to provide my every need and never will!

CHALLENGE

What about you? How can you learn to become more patient? I believe the answer is simple- daily purpose to wholeheartedly seek the Lord until you are content with Him alone as your sole source of love, peace, and satisfaction. I assure you that this is not easy and definitely not a mindless task. Gaining the attribute of true patience is a hard and difficult journey, but though Christ it is achievable and worth every trouble. As I mentioned before, patience is not something we are born with. I am convinced that it comes only from God acting upon one's life. When Christ truly becomes your life, you will begin to trust Him enough to wait on His perfect timing.

Chapter 6

Purity: Desiring What God Desires

Diamonds are rare crystals of high value. Diamonds have grades of various purity. The most rare and valuable diamonds are of extremely high purity. It is not easy to find a pure, flawless diamond. Equally so, people who value their purity enough to fight to protect it are rare. Imagine with me that you are stranded in the middle of Saharan desert and have been for 48 hours. You are only minutes away from dehydration and heat exhaustion when, all of the sudden, you find a table with a two cups of water. One cup is crystal clear and clean-it is pure. The other is utterly filthy-it is defiled. You have a choice. At first, you think it is too good to be true and are debating whether or not you are seeing a mirage or the real thing. Which one would you choose? I do not know a person on earth who would, in their right mind, choose the filth-tainted water over the pure vessel. God desires purity just like we do.

God desires a pure vessel to use to glorify Him. He is the sole initiator and source of purity. In 2 Chronicles 16:9, we learn that the eyes of the Lord run to and fro throughout the whole earth, to show Himself strong in the behalf of them whose heart is perfect towards Him. We understand from this passage that God is seeking out those with hearts perfect or complete towards Him. Since we know that we cannot obtain perfect hearts without being pure, we can come to the conclusion that God is looking for pure people. We therefore, as the children of purity, must commit to becoming and remaining in a constant state of repentance from sin (so that we can remain pure).

The Father of perfection expects His children to strive to be perfect. Jesus says, "Be ye therefore perfect, even as your Father in Heaven is perfect."[1] I know you are probably thinking "but that's impossible! Why would God command for us to be perfect if He knows we are unable to attain perfection?" The word "perfect," in the context of this verse, means to love as God loves: to love without partiality. Despite popular opinion, Christ is clarifying that God's commandment is to love everyone regardless of whether or not they reciprocate love in return. As followers of Christ, we are not promised to be loved by others, but we are loved by God and He commands us to love others as He loves us. Christ loved others unconditionally. You and I are instructed to show the love that we have been shown with everyone. The Father expects that since Christ has given us a new nature, we should strive to live as if we know that we have been purchased by the blood of the righteous King.

In 1 Peter 2:9, God considers us a peculiar people that are set apart to show the praises of Him who has called us out of darkness and into His marvelous light! Before we can completely understand the purity God has called us to, we must fully grasp the complexity of who we were without Christ. We were as that cup of water that has been polluted. We were utterly filthy as a dead, rotting carcass. We were without hope; dead in our trespasses and sins. We were blinded by the lust of the flesh, the lust of the eyes, and the pride of life. Sin was our master. The Bible says that before Christ we were as children of disobedience who walked with the world and were in bondage to sin's destructive power.[2] We indulged in sin alone are were called the children of wrath. This does not sound like a group of individuals that I would want to fellowship with, yet this is who we were as we walked in continual sin. We were children of the wicked one. We were walking blinded and bound by sin, into a Christ-less eternity. That is who we were. Christ saw our sinful, helpless state, left the comforts and perfection of Heaven, came to this sin-saturated world, and died to purify as many as would be willing to repent from sin so that all could have a way to enter into the perfect Heaven through the perfect Son of God.

You see Worthless, He sees Priceless

Madison, a junior in high school was known as a fun-loving, adventure-seeking girl. She loved God. She was raised in church. She had a wonderful relationship with her parents. One day, her family went to a purity conference. She heard that purity was a good thing and that if she would commit to remaining pure for her future husband, God would be pleased with her and bless her exceedingly. Madison was sold. During an exuberant walk down to the altar, Madison decided to remain a virgin by resolving not to "go all the way" sexually until her wedding night with her husband. She was proud of her decision. Her parents were excited about her decision and were extremely supportive. She started *being* the church instead of merely taking up a seat. She got involved. She started inviting her friends and eventually even complete strangers to church. The entire church could see a noticeable change in her life. She felt close to the Lord. She was content with Jesus alone and was as happy as she had ever been.

Is it not amazing how much fulfillment and joy we find in Christ when we are actively living in obedience to what He said? However, this is not where Madison's story ends. Slowly but surely, Madison started making little compromises. A few months later, Madison became determined to get as close to the line of "going too far" without actually crossing it and falling over the cliff. She had already committed to abstinence before marriage, but she was not going to simply sit there as a princess locked up in a castle waiting on her Prince Charming.

She wanted to experience all of the excitement of walking on the edge. You know, the feeling of getting close to danger without getting hurt. She wanted to get the best of both worlds. She wanted one foot on God's side of the line and the other on the world's side. In her mind, and the minds of most people, Madison was still a good girl. Sure, she made bad choices on occasion by compromising certain parts of her purity, but she had not actually "engaged in intercourse." This is an impressive feat as a teenage girl in public school, but she would soon find that the consequences of compromise are devastating. Her compromises started small. A kiss here and there, a longer kiss here and there, a drink here and there, a smoke here and there, but for the most part, she defied the odds and still somehow maintained her testimony among her friends and family. Even though she looked pure, Madison did not feel pure in any way. She felt dirty, defiled, and desolate. She longed for God's presence. She yearned to be close to Him again as she once was. After a little too close to the edge experience with an eighteen-year-old boy, the Lord opened her eyes to just how far she had gone away from Him. She reached her breaking point. She somehow managed to get out of the locked truck door and ran into the woods where she called her parents who immediately rushed to her rescue. In the midst of guilt and shame, she broke into tears and repented of her sins. She turned away from her sins and turned towards her Heavenly Father who welcomed her with open arms.

Miraculously, the Lord had protected her in spite of her carelessness. Today, she is happily married and has three beautiful children. God kept His promise even though she went back on her promise to Him. We serve a faithful God whose faithfulness is not dependent upon our faithfulness to Him. That being said, our fruitfulness through Him is dependent upon our faithfulness to Him. The closer we get to the Faithful One, the more faithful we will naturally become. Decide to be more faithful to purity than you have in the past. Do not let the evil one convince you that you have committed sins that God cannot forgive. Your past is a place of reference, not residence. If you have confessed it, God has forgotten it so you do the same. We must remember that God has forgotten our sin once and for all. Resolve to live from this day forward in the freedom of the Father's forgiveness.

This story is one of redemption. We have all made compromises. We have all fallen short of God's glory.[3] We have not been faithful to God, but He has been faithful to us. Through this time in Madison's life, God changed her perspective. She saw who she thought He was- a lawgiver. She then saw who she was- full of rebellious sin. Finally she saw who God *really* was- her loving Father who is faithful and just to forgive and cleanse her of all sin.[4] Just as God changed Madison's perspective and purified her heart, He desires to change our perspective to one of purity- not merely in our actions alone, but in our thoughts, words, and hearts.

Growing up, I experienced a much different approach to purity than most people. Purity was a necessity. Since God commanded me to be pure, my parents, pastor, and leaders in my life seemingly constantly harped on purity. The message that I perceived was "purity is worth the wait. Abstinence until marriage is God's design for our lives. Having sex whenever you want and with whomever you want may seem exhilarating, but it always leads to destruction." This was what I was taught. This was the culture that I grew up around. I am blessed beyond expression to have been able to have Godly influences in my life to challenge me to do what is right; but as you could imagine, being that I was a teenage boy and all, I needed more proof. Like salvation, I needed to find out for myself that purity and abstinence until marriage was truly worth abandoning all the "fun and adventure found in a little harmless sensuality." After all, this was too important of a subject to merely take their word for it. I started studying God's Word intentionally honing my attention on verses that had to do with purity.

I, like just about every other teenager out there, was trying to find a happy medium. I wanted to honor my parents, impress the Godly leaders placed over me, and still be in good graces with God; all while still dabbling with a little sin here and there so I could enjoy myself. I mean, how could they expect me to remain as celibate as a castaway until the day I say "I do?" I decided that I would attempt to please the Lord while occasionally doing things he abhorred. It seemed like "the best of both worlds" in my mind at the time. I mean, I could do what most proclaimed "Christians" do by doing what momentarily felt good and then just go and "repent" later. What I would quickly discover was that this was not possible. God will not stand idly by while we, as those who claim to be His children, abuse His grace and disgrace His name.

I soon found that this road was very easy to travel up, but more difficult to turn around and go in the other direction. It was like a river. Imagine you and some friends decide to go river tubing one day. The flow of the current swiftly and smoothly travels downstream and everything is so calm and peaceful. Life is fine and dandy until you hear something far in the distance. You lay back down and continue relaxing as you determine that the noise is so far away that it poses no immediate danger and therefore is not a threat. A few minutes later, the current slowly builds speed and tubing takes that turn from relaxation to adventurous excitement. You and your friends are having a fantastic time! Some of your friends are dangerously standing on their tubes with substantially sized rocks all around. You decide to do the same, and start dancing to make them laugh. You are having so much fun that you have all but forgotten about the sound you heard earlier in the distance.

All of the sudden, without much warning, you see that a few hundred yards away, is an upcoming waterfall. Fear suddenly strikes your heart like a baseball bat strikes a ball. You feel as though this is the end of the line. Looks of regret and remorse flush over your face as you yell to your friends "WATERFALL AHEAD!" You anxiously begin to paddle with all the strength your arms can muster, but it is no use. Your "friends", now safely ashore thanks to your warning dare not to attempt to rescue you as they would only be endangering their lives. Some watch in horror as you come closer and closer to the inevitable, insurmountable falls you are rapidly approaching. Others have the nerve to laugh and mock to themselves at the stupidity of your decision to ignorantly disregard the sound you previously heard. As your entire life vividly flashes before your eyes, you plummet head-first into what you know to be sudden death.

This example is one of sin. As we see in the story, there is pleasure in sin. They were all having a great time-but it was, quite literally, short lived. It was only for a season. Sin does not last. It does not satisfy. Sin will take you further than you want to go, keep you longer than you want to stay, and cost you far more than you want to pay. I have discovered this both from experience and from witnessing it in others. God's Word teaches that we cannot serve two masters.[5] We find that we will either truly love one and hate the other or despise the one and hate the other. This brings us to a decision. We must determine in our hearts to be pure by making God our only master, or just to be impure by making this world and the things therein be our only master. According to scripture, we cannot have both.

After a couple romantic flings where I exerted far too much emotionally into the relationship, I decided to live pure in every aspect of my life. Now do not get me wrong, by God's grace, I had never physically defiled myself and am a virgin (a choice that was daily being tested and questioned by those at my public high school), but I had lusted in my heart and mind. Therefore, I was just as equally guilty of committing fornication by Jesus' standards.[6] After sincerely studying God's Word and reading multiple books consisting of *Every young man's battle* by Stephen Arterburn and Fred Stoeker, *I kissed dating goodbye* by Joshua Harris, and *When God writes your love story* by Eric and Leslie Ludy, I decided to stop dating and determine to live a pure life that honors and shows love to my Heavenly Father and my future spouse by giving God the pen to my love story.

This does not mean that I completely stop talking to girls and lock myself in my room with only a Bible and sit there painstakingly denying every one of my desires. That would be miserable and is not the way the Father intended for us to live. I began to live with a renewed desire to know the Father deeper in order to make Him known more effectively to a world who was, unknowingly, desperately seeking Him. I began to think about and pray for my future spouse more than I did for myself. Life was so much more enjoyable when I surrendered complete control to the Father and let Him live in me and love through me to maximum effectiveness. I was far from perfect, but I began to passionately pursue perfection as I pursued purity.

It was a chilly Thursday afternoon and I was anxiously awaiting the arrival of puppies from my dog Piper. I had gone through all the trouble of traveling two hours to take her on a "doggie date" with another purebred chocolate lab and paid the owner for the arrangement. I had been buying and feeding her extra food so that, when she had the puppies, she would be healthy and warm enough to feed and keep them warm. I had been trying my best to keep her put up and away from other male dogs as I would prefer to have pure-breeds instead of mutts. After making all the preparations, I was readily excited about seeing, raising, and most importantly selling them to raise money for my education after high school.

It was a Wednesday and I was rushing around the house trying to get some homework done before I had to leave to pick up kids on the church van. In all of the chaotic stress of trying to figure out what on earth 'x' equals and wondering why some genius ever created a class as difficult as advanced algebra and trigonometry, the church van pulled up and started honking the horn. I had lost track of time. In a hectic frenzy, I shot off the couch and ran to go help pick people up for church. Unfortunately I forgot about Piper and accidentally left her out of her pen. When we got home that evening, she was nowhere to be found. I searched frantically for her about an hour before going inside to thaw out from the cold.

Knowing that she could have her puppies any day now, all I could do was hope and pray that she was somewhere safe, warm, and comfortable. The next morning I got up and she had still not shown up. After school, I came home to find Piper still missing from amidst her mother and grandmother. The following day, were the exact same results. Finally, when I arrived home from high school and started shouting her name, she surprisingly came out and snuggled up to me as she always greeted me. I instantly thanked the Lord for bringing her home safe and sound. As I was petting her, I noticed that something was different about her- she had lost a ton of weight! It was at that moment that I heard a faint noise of whining close by. I began to thank the Lord yet again for His goodness.

I lured Piper into the garage and eagerly went to see the newborns. I anxiously picked one up and to my utter surprise, it was not a chocolate lab. It was black with white on the chest. Apparently, Piper had snuck away without me knowing it and the puppies were not from the other lab as I planned. I was initially devastated and disgusted at the sight of them. But then I became guilty of thinking such a thought and lovingly cradled them in my arms and thanked God for teaching me such a valuable lesson. All life is a precious miracle from the Creator. God has a unique plan that He has specifically designated for every living creature. As I pondered why God would allow such a thing to happen and what He was trying to teach me through this situation, the following truth continued to come up in my mind- *God makes no mistakes.* God thought to teach me in that moment a lesson that was more important than me making extra money for my education.

Isaiah 55:5 tells us that the Lord's thoughts are not our thoughts and His ways are not our ways. The next verse, though less quoted and less popular, contains a vital word that makes a huge difference- *higher.* The thoughts and ways of the Almighty are infinitely higher than our own. We cannot understand why He allows certain things to happen and why He does what He does. This causes us to trust Him completely. Our only other choice is to become angry and remain in a state of confusion.

In the same way that I was originally disappointed that the puppies I was expecting to be pure were impure, God prefers and expects purity from His children. He wants us to desire what He desires. God is pure and His standards for us are that we strive to be pure. We can be pure through Christ's blood. We will still continue to sin on occasion, but we can be sure that when we sin His love for us is not affected in the least. The Father loves His children with an unconditional love. When I found out that Piper had been sneaking around and ended up with impure pups, do you think I stopped loving her? Of course not! In a similar way, God does not stop loving us simply because we fail to comply with His standards. However, He is disappointed in us as He expects us to uphold His commands with the highest esteem and do our best to live in accordance to them. Simply because God does not love us any less when we fail, does not give us any excuse whatsoever to sin freely. A true follower of Christ desires to be free from sin, not to sin freely.

Once we encounter the God of purity, we will begin to desire purity with all that is within us. Christ's purity inspires us to be pure. If we are in Him, we are purified through Him. You see, God desires to use a pure vessel. In the same way that you, given the choice, would choose a pure drink in contrast to contaminated one, God will choose to use pure over impure. If you claim to be pure, you are rare. I have never met anyone like you before and am doubtful that I ever will. If you have somehow discovered how to remain untainted in this sex-crazed, sin-filled world, you are one in a million. Keep striving to remain pure in your thoughts, words, and actions by seeking the Designer of Purity Himself.

For those who are impure, there is hope! Everyone was once impure and everyone can become pure through Christ's blood. What is the secret to becoming pure? The answer is simple. In fact, it is so simple that most people do not even believe it. The secret to how you can be pure is to ask God. The Bible says, "If we confess our sins, he is faithful and just to forgive us our sins and cleanse us from all unrighteousness"[7]. The good news is that God recreates you pure each time you, in faith, ask Him. Of course, we will still fall short of God's perfect standard of perfection, but when we do, Jesus Christ becomes our mediator to the Father. He intercedes on our behalf. He claims "they are pure because I am pure and they are in me; they are mine."

Challenge

What about you? Are you attempting to script your own "happily ever after"? I challenge you to relinquish control of your futile attempts to discover love by discovering The Author of love in a way that you never have before. Let the source of purity itself cleanse you through the blood of Jesus Christ. Nothing you have done can keep God from loving more and nothing you could do could make Him love you any less than He already does. You are never beyond the reach of God's forgiveness. Whatever you have done or failed to do in the past, you can claim the promises God gives to forgive and forget your sin once you have repented. Take God's Word for it, you will not regret it.

> "For he that is dead is freed from sin. Now if we be dead with Christ, we believe that we shall also live with him: Knowing that Christ being raised from the dead dieth no more; death hath no more dominion over him. For in that he died, he died unto sin once: but in that he liveth, he liveth unto God. Likewise reckon ye also yourselves

to be dead indeed unto sin, but alive unto God through Jesus Christ our Lord. Let not sin therefore reign in your mortal body, that ye should obey it in the lusts thereof. Neither yield ye your members as instruments of unrighteousness unto sin: but yield yourselves unto God, as those that are alive from the dead, and your members as instruments of righteousness unto God. For sin shall not have dominion over you: for ye are not under the law, but under grace." Romans 6:7-14

Chapter 7

Prayer: Discovering the Power of Talking to God

What is prayer? Let's just face it, prayer gets a bad rap. I constantly hear people say that praying feels as if they are merely talking to themselves. Many of Christ's proclaimed followers complain that God never answers their prayer requests and that makes them doubt if God is even listening to their prayers in the first place. Perhaps you have said similar things or at least thought them.

Prayer is simply talking to God. Prayer is simple, but it is not always easy. Prayer is the essential lifeline of a believer. To be a Christian without prayer is like a car without gas. In the same way that a car cannot accomplish its purpose, someone who claims to follow Christ without constant communication with the Father cannot do anything of lasting value. A prayerless Christian is void of power. This is exactly what Satan wants! He wants followers of Christ to be powerless so that we are unable to truly do anything for Christ, but let me urge you now to look at this section with an open mind and consider how you may improve your prayer life today.

God has much to say about prayer in His Word. Here are just a few interesting facts about prayer. Fifty five percent of Americans claim to pray every day, according to a *2014 Pew Research Center survey*, while twenty one percent say they pray weekly leaving only a mere twenty three percent who say they seldom or never pray. In the same survey, sixty-three percent of proclaimed Christians in the U.S. say praying regularly is an essential part of their Christian identity. There are a total of six-hundred and fifty prayers listed in the Bible. There are approximately four-hundred and fifty recorded answers to prayer in the Bible. Jesus is recorded praying twenty-five times during His earthly ministry. Although prayer can be done from any bodily position, The Bible lists five specific postures: sitting[1], standing[2], kneeling[3], face down to the ground[4], and finally with hands lifted up[5].

As I am currently writing about prayer, I am reminded of an elderly widow in my church who has little means of providing for herself. Her husband died suddenly leaving her with a house and a substantial amount of debt. She claims to have just enough money to buy food and gas to get to church and back. Every week that I see her, she persistently reminds me to cut her grass. The county keeps sending her letters threatening to fine her if she cannot keep her grass below a certain number of inches. I am typically really busy from traveling to preach and work in other states to doing odd jobs to raise money for Bible College, so this was an inconvenience many times. However, the constant nagging of the widow always compelled me to go cut her grass even though it costed me more money than she could pay. If I am willing to grant the request of a widow I barely know, how much more is God willing to give good things to His children who ask Him in faith! God wants to bless you beyond your wildest imagination, but you must be willing to surrender all to Him and trust Him completely!

We have probably heard on more than one occasion that there is power in prayer, but how many of us have actually experienced this so called "power" firsthand? Followers of Christ (myself included) are often guilty of overusing the phrase "I'm praying for you." To be completely honest, there have been dozens of times that I have told an individual "I will be praying for you" and never did. Whether I was simply too busy and did not have time, or I completely forgot; I promised those people I would lift them up in prayer before the Father and I failed to do so. I have since learned from my mistakes and whenever I am asked to pray for someone, I will immediately stop whatever it is that I am doing and start praying for them right then and there. This eliminates the temptation to forget which shows that I really do not care about the person who cared enough to ask for prayer.

There is a common misconception about prayer. Prayer is often viewed as a "give me" request. We only look at what we can ask God for a His provision in our desire. True prayer is so much more than asking and receiving things, and when we really understand prayer and our heart is in the right place we will not think of prayer in this light. In fact, those who think prayer is about what they can get from God should not be surprised when they do not receive an answer. God is not our personal genie. He does not live in a lamp that we rub when we want or need something. On the contrary, the God of the Bible is far more than our little personal "prayer answerer." Sadly, I would dare to say that this is the perspective that most people have of God. I might have mentioned this previously in the book before, but I am going to say it again-God does not exist for us. We exist for Him. Without Him creating us in the first place, we would not exist. Take a moment and think about that previous phrase. When we approach God, we are to have a knowledge of who exactly it is that we are approaching. When a believer prays, they are talking to the omnipotent God of Heaven.

It is vital for us to remember that God is the Creator, but it is just as equally important for us to realize that the God who we are talking to is not a distant Creator who has no affiliation with His creation. Rather, God is a loving Father and righteous Judge. If you are saved by Christ's grace and through faith in His finished work on the cross and in the grave, then God is your Heavenly Father! How awesome it is that we who were previously pronounced enemies of God are now saints justified by Jesus Christ.[6] Through Christ, we have unlimited access to the Father.[7]

In order to have a proper understanding of the relationship we have with The Father, we need to take a look at one of the most famous of Jesus' parables; which is most commonly referred to as "The Story of the Prodigal Son" (Luke 15). Notice with me that there are two petitions that Jesus gives us in this parable.

There are several evident truths that we can learn from this story. First of all, notice with me that the Bible is clear that the prodigal son is indeed a child of the Father—regardless of the carefree decisions he made, he never stopped being the Father's Son. Therefore we can infer that his identity was found in whom he belonged, the father, not in his actions. The fact that his identity never changed is important for you and I to remember as well. Those of us who are children of the Father are not defined by what we do, but by what has been done for us through Christ. It is in Christ alone that our identity, hope, peace, strength, and life is found. The younger son grew tired of waiting for his father to die so that he could receive his inheritance. So one day the younger son mustered up the audacity to demand that the father give him the "the portion of goods that falleth to me" as mentioned in verse twelve. The meaning behind this disrespectful petition was something along the line of "I wish you were dead already so I could have your treasure. I do not care about you to the extent that I am not even willing to wait until you die to receive what is rightfully mine. Give me what I would already have if you were in the ground." Sounds pretty harsh to me. Imagine the way this made the father feel. The father raised, rebuked, and instructed his son and this was the result. The father loved his son and knew this was not a good decision, but his son had a free will to choose therefore the father granted his request. I think it is needful for us to notice the small word "*them*" in verse twelve. When the younger son asked for his portion of goods, the father divided his living unto both of his sons. In verse thirteen, we see that only a few days after the younger son got what he wanted, he gathered up his riches and went on a road trip to a different country far from home. While he was on his little pleasure trip, the Bible says that he "wasted his substance with riotous living." Now if you are like me, you are probably wondering what exactly the word *riotous* means. According to Webster's dictionary, the first definition of the word means "a disturbance of the peace." A riotous person is also considered one who "incites or takes part in a riot." A riotous person is also "loose, wanton, or marked by unrestrained revelry." We can associate this son with the typical lost college student who is enjoying the temporary pleasures of their youth. He most likely compromised his purity with a harlot and got drunk every night for several weeks. His nights were undoubtedly filled with partying and sex. He appeared to have what the world would describe as "the life." He was a young and wealthy man. He had no need to work or any desire to do anything meaningful. This son had no worries or cares in the world. He probably thought his money would last him forever and he would die an old man with a life lived full of fun and pleasure. But unknown to this son, sin is temporary. The fun and pleasure would soon end. He would run out of money and his supposed "friends" would leave him. The lovers that he had spent so many long and pleasurable nights with wanted nothing to do with him once he went bankrupt. This once popular total-package of a guy was now a broke bum forced to find work wherever it could be found. There was a famine in the land and food was as scarce as there are trees in the Arabian Desert. He found himself feeding pigs and even eating of their slop. In verse sixteen the Bible adds the phrase, "and no man gave unto him," as a sort of reminder to us that when we turn to the world seeking satisfaction we will always end up empty handed. The son was now at the lowest of the lows. Jews were instructed in the Bible to have no affiliation with pigs. If any Jew were to touch or eat any part of the pig then they would be considered unclean. The son had hit the bottom of the barrel. I have found this to be true by approaching strangers in the mall in a conversation about Jesus. I have heard countless times by untold amounts of people that sin does not bring lasting satisfaction. I have looked into the eyes of dozens of individuals as they told me through red, tear-stained eyes that sin is never worth it. This once prestigious son now found himself a prodigal son. In verse seventeen through nineteen, we read about how when the son came to his senses. He realized that even the servants in his father's house had more than enough bread to eat, yet he was barely surviving by dining with the pigs. He concluded that if he went to his father and repented then perhaps he could at least serve his father as a hired servant and survive. This son knew that he was no longer worth of sonship, but at his low and desperate state he would do anything. What happened next surprised everyone. The Bible says in verse twenty that "he arose, and came to his father. But when he was a long way off, his father saw him, and had compassion, and ran, and fell on his neck, and kissed him". In verse 21 the son spoke to his father saying, "Father, I have sinned against Heaven, and in thy sight, and am no more worthy to be called thy son." Pay careful attention to the father's response. The Father, without saying a word to his son, summoned his servants and said, "bring forth the best robe, and put it on him; and put a ring on his hand, and shoes on his feet: and bring hither the fatted calf, and kill it; and let us eat, and be merry. For this my son was dead, and is alive again; he was lost, and is found. And they began to be merry."

The son showed no compassion toward his father, yet the father showed compassion on him. The son did not deserve compassion, but that did not alter the father's actions in any way. He forgave the unworthy son. He clothed him with the best robe. He gave him a ring. He put shoes on his feet. He allowed the best calf; the most delicately delicious and tenderized meat in all of his household, to be slain. As we discuss the importance of each act of the father in this parable, I want us to put ourselves in the shoes of the prodigal son. Before we can truly grasp the gravity of what it means to have fellowship with the Father in Heaven, we must identify ourselves with a prodigal. We have all sinned against our Heavenly Father and every time we do it is equivalent to what is being done by this prodigal. Jesus' parable is an example of our relationship with God once we sin after we are His child.

Imagine this scene. We were the prodigal. God is the Father. We have sinned against Him. We have chosen to treat Him as if he were unimportant to us by leaving Him and turning to the world of sin. We have chosen to take the bodies that He has given us and waste them until we are eating with some of the lowest of God's creation. We are at our lowest. We have expended every ounce of worth we had been given. We are miserable. We are destitute to the point of embarrassment. We have been forsaken by those who once called us friends. The world that promised endless happiness and pleasure has rewarded us with only emptiness and confusion. We can go no lower and we can smell no worse. Our stench has exceeded the stench of our companion's hairless piglets. In the midst of our filth, a slight glimmer of hope is remembered. Only when we are at our lowest do we realize our helpless condition and look to the Highest. We figure that, although we no longer deserve to be His child anymore, becoming his hired servant is much better that starving with animals! So we go, with heads down and in shame to The One who has given us life before we threw it away. We are hurting, helpless, and hopeless. We expect to be treated as we deserve by the Righteous Father. We lift our eyes in excruciating humiliation, contemplating what we will say to the Life Giver. As we debate whether to lie and tell Him that someone stole our treasure, we instantly rule that out as we remember that He is much too wise and holy for lies. After brainstorming a few more possible explanations, we realize that every excuse is eliminated. With tears in our eyes and regret in our hearts, we are surprised to see our Father running towards us from a long ways off. We would run towards him, but our sinful lifestyle has left us void of nourishment for several days and we are barely able to keep walking. When we finally encounter each other, the Father responds much differently than we previously anticipated. In compassion, the Father joyfully welcomes us home with a warm embrace. As we are in the middle of humbly confessing our faults, failures, and unworthiness to be called His child, He interrupts us by telling his servants to get the best robe in the house, a ring for our hand, and shoes for our feet. The robe represents the righteousness of Christ. This signifies to all that we are His children. The ring symbolizes our loyalty and identification as a royal child of the King of Kings and Lord of Lords. The shoes represent a solid foundation that is built on Him alone. Last of all, as a result of our repentance from sin, the Father allows His best to be slain in return for a celebration of our new life. In order for the ceremony of celebration for our new life, blood must be shed. I believe that the Father in the parable offering His best to be slain for the good of those at the feast is Christ foreshadowing how God the Father offered His best to be slain for the good of any who choose to come to the feast at The Father's house. This, however, is not verified truth as it is merely a rough interpretation of what I believe Christ was symbolizing in this particular portion of scripture. It is evident in verse twenty four that the reason for all of this was because we were dead and are now alive! We were lost and are now found!

You who are reading this book are either lost or found. Are you a prodigal who is still lost, exploring in the world of sin? You hope that it will bring lasting satisfaction, but the truth is that it will not bring any satisfaction. Maybe you are now saved and were once lost. For those who may still be lost, sin does not provide the satisfaction that it promises. You know deep down inside that temporary pleasure high's only leave you with a cheap substitute for temporary amusement. Sin only leaves you feeling defiled, discontented, and disoriented. You are yearning for something real; something genuinely satisfying. Something that is deeper than temporary delight. Something that will give you peace, rest, and everlasting fulfillment. The something you are looking for is actually Someone. He is the Father who has given you the gift of life. You have wasted, abused, and violated it thus far. You have fallen into the trap of thinking that drugs, alcohol, and sexual activity outside of the bounds of God's definition of marriage will fill the void that only the Father is able to fill. You have learned from experience that transgressing God's laws does not satisfy. So why not give Him a try? Why not submit to obedience of His Word? You have tried fornication. You have tried drugs. You have tried alcohol. You have tried dead religion. Each of these things result in death. None of those things fulfilled the longing in your soul for satisfaction. So you continue to seek and will find that nothing other than your Creator can truly satisfy you. The time has come for you to decide to stop relentlessly pursuing vain pleasures and trust Jesus. Once you decide to trust Christ completely, nothing else even comes close in comparison.

As we continue in Christ's parable, we discover that his older brother was returning from a long day working in the field. The older brother was curious to know the cause of this celebration. When he inquired of a servant and found out that the sacrifice was in celebration for his brother coming home safely, the Bible says that he was angry and refused to even come inside and partake in the celebration. The father went out to him and asked what was wrong. The older brother responded by telling his father that he had faithfully served for many years and never sinned against any commands. He went on to remind his father that his younger brother had devoured his own substance with harlots and sinners. He then started complaining that he had never received anything for his faithful service, yet his brother was rewarded with the best calf for his rebellion. The father responds by telling him that he will always be with him and everything that he owns belongs to him. He tells the older son that there was nothing wrong with celebrating the return of the prodigal son and that they should be glad that he who was once dead is now alive!

Perhaps you are more inclined to act like the older brother. Many times I have struggled, and still struggle today, with my inclination to act as the older brother. It is a common manifestation among many veteran followers of Christ. We tend to judge and even become angry at those who have indulged in sin their entire lives and then repent and receive forgiveness. For instance, a person like myself who has been raised in Christian home is typically less likely to rejoice at the repentance of a sinner than a recently saved individual. Statistics have proven this to be true, but statistics are not always correct. If you tend to act in a similar way to the older son when one who was lost becomes found, you can change. You must change. Remember way back to when God saved you. You were lost and in a helpless state until God saved you. You were once dead and are now alive. You were once a sinner and are now a saint. When we are tempted to act in a less than enthusiastic way when someone is born again, choose to join the psalmist by remembering the joy of your salvation.[8]

By reading this parable of Jesus, we can learn how we ought to listen and respond to God. God is our Heavenly Father. Our Father loves us and wants to have a personal relationship with us. The most important ingredient in a healthy relationship is communication. For example, my family and I would not have a strong relationship if we never spoke. We would have a feeling of closeness because we live in the same vicinity, but if we rarely spoke, our relationship would be awkward to say the least. In a similar way, God wants a strong, lasting, and enriching relationship with you and I that results in the production of fruit for Him. In order for this to take place we must make time to listen to Him and speak to Him. The longer we go without communication the more awkward and more difficult the interaction will be. Be diligent and faithful in your prayer time! It will benefit you more than you know.

The idea of prayer can seem awkward at times. It can sometimes feel as if we are talking to ourselves. This feeling has been present in my life at times and sadly, I stopped praying for a while. This feeling of awkwardness is an obvious reminder that we are not as close to God as we should be. I started hungering and thirsting to know God more. I wanted to learn more about God and get closer to Him. An amazing thing happened- I grew closer to God. Prayer became less awkward as God became more real to me. This is the way prayer should work- when we hear from God, it is only expected that we respond to God. Martin Luther once been said that "To be a Christian without prayer is no more possible than to be alive without breathing". There is much truth in that statement. Prayer is not merely an "essential part" of our relationship with God, but the very life of our relationship with Him.

Challenge

How deep is your prayer life? Do you feel as if you talk to God as your Father who created you, loves you, and wants to hear from you or a monarchical ruler that has no time for you? God formed you in your mother's womb. He knows infinitely more about you than anyone else on earth; more than you actually know about yourself. This same God has spoken to you in His Word. How have you responded to what the Father has said? Perhaps you know little about this loving Father. He has clearly revealed Himself in His Word. You must decide to put aside every distraction and purpose in your heart that you will get more serious about your prayer life. Procrastination will be your biggest enemy. There will always be plenty of excuses, but will you let those excuses control you? There is no excuse that is worthy of you not spending time with the Father in prayer. If you want to grow close to God, you must make it a priority to spend time with Him. You must determine if God is a worthy investment of your time. Are you willing to spend time with the Father?

Chapter 8

Price: What is the Cost of Following Christ?

Jesus approached two men who were casting nets into the water as they always did. As fishermen, it was their job to catch fish. One day, they encountered Jesus and their lives were changed forever. Jesus said, "Follow me, and I will make you fishers of men."[1] The response these men had would determine the rest of their lives and eternity. Imagine with me if you will that they rejected Christ's offer. Why should they follow Him? This man was a stranger. Typically young men would choose to study under a Rabbi who would teach them skills and wisdom that they could apply to their lives. It was very unusual for Jesus, being a teacher, to choose people to follow Him. It normally is not a good idea to leave behind everything to follow a stranger, but as these fishermen would soon discover, this was the single greatest decision of their lives. Although they did not know Him, they were willing to immediately leave the comfort of their nets and follow.

People might say that their circumstances are different, but are our circumstances really that different from the disciples in the New Testament? Notice that they left something behind. The cost for these men were what we might initially deem insignificant, yet in reality, they left behind their livelihood. Imagine if Jesus asked you to quit your job and become a foreign, church planting missionary. Would you be willing to pay the price to follow Christ or is the cost too high? To what extent do you trust God? Are you willing to abandon the temporary comforts of this world in return for the everlasting satisfaction that Christ provides?

These men chose to give up everything in order to follow Him. They found that in Christ resides the everlasting satisfaction that no amount of money, sex, family, or any other worldly pleasures can provide. They were willing to give their lives as the payment for following Christ. Each of them sacrificed everything to follow Christ. They all eventually paid the ultimate price by dying as martyrs. History records that Simon Peter, after years of faithful service, was martyred in Rome under the reign of Emperor Nero. Peter supposedly inquired of the Romans to be crucified upside down so that his death would not be equivalent to Jesus and the Romans allegedly obliged.

The apostle Peter suffered a cruel and violent death as a result of his work for Christ. Peter was not the first martyr of Christ and most certainly not the last.

Andrew was an apostle of Christ and the brother of Peter who also suffered a torturous death for the cause of Christ. According to Dorman Newman, a 15th century religious historian, Andrew went to a city in Western Greece called Petras in 69 AD. There he debated religion with Roman proconsul Aegeates. Aegeates attempted to convince Andrew to forsake Christ, for if he did not, Aegeates promised to torture and execute him. Andrew refused to forsake Christ, therefore Aegeates decided to give Andrew the full treatment. Andrew was brutally scourged and beaten. He was also tied to a cross instead of nailed because it put the victims in more pain and agony. For two days Andrew slowly bled out, all while continuing to preach the Gospel of the Lord Jesus Christ with all of his strength to each and every person who passed by him.

The Bible gives account in Acts 12:1-9 that James (the brother of John) was killed with the sword. As history conveys, the newly-appointed governor of Judea, Herod Agrippa, decided to integrate himself with the Romans by seeking, torturing, and executing all the leaders of the new Christian faith. After James was arrested and found guilty by Jewish and Roman law, he was led to the place of his execution. Inspired by the fearless courage and determination to follow Christ until his death, James' unnamed accuser repented and converted to Christ. Even in death, James was a bold witness to Jesus Christ.

You may be wondering, "Did not John get to live an easy rest of his life and die a peaceful death?" Well, it is a common misconception that John got off scot-free and never suffered any persecution. According to Tertullian (*The Prescription of Heretics)*, John was said to have been banished (presumably to the island of Patmos) after being plunged into boiling oil in Rome and suffering nothing from it. It is said that everyone in the audience of Colosseum were converted to Christianity upon witnessing this miracle. So the apostle John died a peaceful death... after being thrown in scalding hot oil alive and exiled to the isle of Patmos; an island prison for outlaws. God miraculously preserved his life so he could write the book of Revelation.

Each of them endured tremendous amounts of pain as a result of their decision follow The Messiah- no matter the cost. If we are willing to follow Christ, we ought to expect no less than the same. How about you? What amount of persecution have you suffered for Christ's sake?

It is a privilege to follow Christ. He is calling all people to abandon all and follow Him, but few are willing to pay the price. In Matthew 19, Jesus encounters the rich young ruler. This man was religious and devoted, but he was not a follower of Christ. When this man asked Jesus how to inherit eternal life, Jesus commanded him to sell all of his possessions and follow Him. The rich young ruler was not willing to pay the price for following Christ, and went away sorrowful.

You see, Jesus wanted the rich young ruler to follow Him. Jesus wanted his heart, but this man's eyes were so blinded by his possessions that he could not see the truth of Jesus' call. Jesus was calling him to remove the temptation of riches and give his entire heart to Christ. Today, Jesus does not need or want your money. Money is merely a tool; an optical illusion that temporarily makes you feel safe. God has more riches than anyone could ever possess or even conceive possible. God wants your heart. When He has your heart, you will want to use any money He allows you to have to further the Kingdom of God. Where is your heart today? Does Christ truly have your heart?

Christ's command has not changed. He wants us to surrender all to Him. It is only when we come to the point of total surrender that we will truly experience what it means to follow Christ. The Lord does not need your money. Your meager possessions and futile trinkets are of no importance to the Father. You must understand that even the street of Heaven is made of pure gold. God does not want your money. He wants your heart. When He truly has your heart, you will both willingly and joyfully give your money for the advancement of His Kingdom. Does The Lord truly have your heart?

You may be thinking "well those were Christ's disciples. It would be easy for someone who actually saw Jesus to pay such a high price for refusing to deny

His name." Christ's closest earthly companions were not the only ones to pay a price for choosing to follow Christ. Even today in the 21st century people suffer persecution for the cause of Christ.

Christ is Worth the Cost

It was a beautiful, sunny day in the heart of what is now known as the Republic of the Congo. The village was filled with life. Children were running, dancing, and singing. There was a peaceful atmosphere. The Chief of the village had gathered the majority of the village together to teach them from a Bible that a missionary had translated into their language. They sang and danced in praise to the amazing newfound love of God they had recently discovered. All of the sudden, war horns sounded without warning. Panic immediately filled the air as gunshots were heard all around the camp. A rival tribe invaded the village seeking more resources. The rival tribe was amazed when this previously violent tribe did not fight back. Genuinely confused, they confronted the chief who told them about how they had discovered a God who taught that love and forgiveness are better than violence and hatred. He told the invaders of the wonderful life in Christ.

The hostile visitors, intrigued by this new discovery, were eager to test the strength of their faith. They lined all the inhabitants of the village into a row and threatened to shoot any that made a noise. Additionally, they took the chief and stripped him of what little clothing he had, and publicly humiliated him in front of his people. When they asked him to give a response to such humiliation, he said "Christ was willing to be stripped of His righteousness so that I may have eternal life in Heaven. It is an honor to be humiliated for Christ's sake. Thank you for giving me the opportunity to great reward in Heaven.

The chief and villagers in the story gave up everything for Christ. How much have you given up for Christ? Jesus Christ is worthy of momentary discomfort for everlasting fulfillment. Christians today, especially in America, do not react to Jesus the same way as these villagers. Is Jesus Christ really worth everything? When each of us truly collide with this Jesus then all of our priorities change and no price is too much to follow Him.

Have You Collided with the King?

It was a warm summer Sunday afternoon when my brother and with three other friends piled into the truck as I drove to the lake where we would have a wonderful time fishing and swimming. Yet, we were unaware that these memories would cause more reflection than a simple day of fellowship. We had an incredible time. None of our three friends has ever caught a fish before this day. Joy and pride swelled up inside each of them as they pulled the fish from the depths of the lake. After catching a few each we got into the boat and went on a boat-ride around the lake.

When we returned we continued fishing for a few hours and then headed back to my brother's truck where we embarked on the journey of taking them home to shower and get dressed for church. I was driving because Logan was still under eighteen and could not carry more than two non-family members. Before we left I made sure everyone was buckled (a decision I thank the Lord for). We were enjoying the beautiful day while listening to some nice Christian music with the windows down. A few minutes down the road, out of nowhere, a car suddenly pulls out in front of me without warning. I had less than a second to react and smashed into the back right corner of the car. Immediately after colliding with the car we ran straight into a wooden telephone pole.

Everyone in the truck instantly panicked and ran as fast and far away from the totaled vehicle in fear that it might explode. Surprisingly, by the grace of God, no one suffered any life-threatening injuries. The woman driving the car apparently did not see the stop sign and did not even bother slowing down. Her mistake quite possibly could have killed all of us. No one from our vehicle would have made it out alive if God had not protected us. From this day forward whenever I hear the word collide I will automatically associate that wreck with the most intense car collision I ever experienced. I can assure you that no one who left the scene that day left with a spirit of indifference or apathy.

Many proclaimed Christians in today's society want just enough of Christ to identify themselves with Him, but when he becomes a serious inconvenience to them they turn away. You and I must decide right now whether Christ is worth surrendering everything for. Can you live as a Christian with one foot in Christ and one foot in the world? Can you live as a Christian if you are living in ongoing rebellion to God's Word? Can you continue to use Christ's forgiveness as a tool and excuse to live life how you want? If you answer "Yes" to any or all of these questions then one day you will be in for a rude awakening. There is not one instance in the Bible where anyone who encountered the Jesus of the Bible left indifferent. Those who collided with Christ in scripture always either responded in radical abandonment and obedience to Him, or utter rejection and rebellion against Him. The same is true for us today. We must decide to, like Elijah, stop halting between two opinions and choose to follow the Lord.[2]

What Does it Mean to Truly Follow Christ?

Truly following Christ is the absolute relinquishing of one's desires and body to the King's service. The Bible says, "What? Know ye not that your body is the temple of the Holy Ghost which is in you, which ye have of God, and ye are not your own? For ye are bought with a price: therefore glorify God in your body and in your spirit, which are God's."[3] If we are to follow the Christ of the Bible, it will require the total abandonment of our lives. This means that our hands are no longer our hands to touch what we want. Our feet are no longer our feet to go where we want. Our mouths are no longer our mouths to say what we want. Our ears are no longer our ears to listen to what we want. Our eyes are no longer our eyes to see what we want. Our minds are no longer our minds to think what we want. Our hearts are no longer our hearts to follow after the things we want. A follower of Christ makes Christ his or her life. Christ becomes our entire purpose and motivation of life. Christ had many fans, but few followers. The realization that individually we are not our own is essential to being a real follower of Christ. Are you willing to make Christ your life?

There is an eternal difference between claiming to be a Christian and genuinely following Christ. There are billions of people all around the world (including many professed "Christians") who truly believe they are on their way to Heaven when they are not relying on Christ alone for salvation. Many proclaimed Christians are basing their eternal destination on good works that they have done. I started asking fellow peers, who I knew were lost, at school this question: "If you stood before Almighty God in an hour, and He asked 'Why should I, who am holy and just in all my ways, let you who have fallen short my standard of perfection by disobeying my laws, into my Heaven' What would your answer be?" Unsurprisingly to me, I received answers such as "I'm not sure, I've never really given it much thought." "Shut the (insert choice word here) up you little (insert choice word here)! I don't give a (insert choice word here) about you or your religion" "Do you really want to know what I would say you little (insert choice word here)? If I stood before your imaginary God I would tell Him I do not want to go to Heaven." After each response, I at least attempted to share the gospel with the broken, hurting, soul underneath the mask. I explained that I, like them, did not care about myself or my religion or I would not have cared enough about them to go out of my way to ask them about their eternal destination. Most of these attempts may have seemed futile at the time, but I built a few relationships with those who truly desired to know more.

After hearing those expected answers I asked the same question to those of my friends who claimed to be followers of Christ. To my utter amazement I heard responses along the lines of "I'm a good person, I've never killed anyone so I deserve to go to Heaven." "I believe in God. I've read the Bible before, so that merits me everlasting life" "Well, I would begin to explain to God that my parents and grandparents were Christians so since I was born into a Christian home, that automatically makes me a Christian." Shocked and in disbelief, I then started asking the same question to adults in church. Nothing could have prepared me for the burden that overwhelmed me once I listened to multiple well-meaning, respected, veteran, church-goers tell me things like "I've been a member of this church for 20+ years and God will not forget my faithfulness to His house." "Well I remember saying a prayer way back when I was younger and God knows my heart." "I have fed the homeless, cared for widows, and given money to orphans. I have served God for all these years and He will one-day reward me with everlasting life! What a day it will be when we see Jesus!"

After receiving each response I was heartbroken because of the percentage of people who had answers that started with "I." I cannot get to Heaven on my own. You cannot get to Heaven on your own. Everlasting life is not a goal to be achieved, but a gift to be received by faith in Christ alone. The Infallible Word of God is clear that Jesus Christ is the only way to Heaven. John 14:6 says, "Jesus saith unto him, 'I am the way, the truth, and the life: no man cometh to the Father, but by me." Notice carefully with me that there is nothing we can do to enter the pearly gates of Heaven. Stop trying to save yourself. To illustrate this I man going to use something I hate with a deep passion. Math. The common denominator is that we all want to go to Heaven. The question is how do we get to Heaven? The Bible says there is only one way to Heaven; the only way is through Jesus Christ.[4] We cannot "be good enough" or "work hard enough" to get to Heaven. Let's use addition to illustrate what many legalist rely on for salvation.

1. Jesus + works= salvation: To what extent are you involved in and serving the church? Are you a good person? Do you help the poor and sick? Do you sacrifice your time and money? What do you do that merits "goodness" for your life?
2. Jesus + baptism= salvation: Have you been baptized? What was the date of your baptism?
3. Jesus + evangelism= salvation: Have you lead any souls to Christ in the past month? Are you a witness to people on an everyday basis? Do you share your faith with other people? Are you doing your part in spreading the Gospel?

Legalism is the doctrine that salvation is attained through good works. Legalists trust in Jesus, but they do not believe that trust alone is enough. Legalists cannot comprehend that Jesus Christ is the only way to Heaven. Legalism traps us into believing that we can contribute to or earn our salvation by our own merits. The Word of God is clear that salvation is solely by grace, through faith in Jesus Christ.[5] Attempting to do good works as a result of Christ saving us is like receiving an immeasurable amount of money from an unknown person and trying, in vain, to pay them back. We owed a debt that we could not pay. Christ paid a debt He did not owe. He paid our sin debt in full. Our attempts to pay for the free gift of salvation are futile.

Works do not equal salvation, but when we are truly saved we will desire to produce goods works as a result of all that Christ has done for us. We cannot earn salvation by working but once we are saved then we will want to actively live in obedience to Christ's commands.

The correct answer to the equation is this: Jesus + nothing = salvation. God's Word is explicitly clear that salvation is not a goal to be achieved, but a gift to be received. It will leave you feeling discontent and always seeking to do more. We will want to continually work for Jesus due to the overwhelming mercy and grace He gives through the free gift of salvation. Work will never be enough to achieve salvation, but salvation works; meaning that once we are saved we will want to work for Him. Authentic holiness is empowered by grace working in us and comes from a strong desire to stay close to the One we love. Truly following Christ is the complete surrendering of your will to His just as He completely surrendered His will to the Father.

As we freely submit ourselves to God His desires will become our desires. The things in which we previously found pleasure in will no longer satisfy our new hearts. When Christ saves us He transforms us from our old sinful creature to an entirely new creation.[6] Somewhere along the line, we have missed what it truly means to follow Christ with our entire lives.

There was once a man known as Mr. Frank. He grew up in a Christian home with parents who both went to church. As a result he genuinely believed he was going to Heaven on account of His parents. He then got involved in the bus ministry and became a bus driver. When he moved to California for work he started attending a church and heard a clear presentation of the Gospel. At the end of the service he realized his need of a Savior and trusted Christ alone for salvation. Mr. Frank now drives the church van for my church and picks up teenagers who would otherwise not come to church at all. I am the bus captain, and together we have seen dozens of souls come to a saving knowledge of Christ!

The story of Mr. Frank is similar to one that I have heard countless times. There are real people who really believe that their eternity rests in either their own merit or the merit of another. There is a real Hell and a real Heaven. There is a real God and a real devil. You and I must make real decisions to tell real people about a real God who loves them enough to die for real sin so that they do not have to go to a real Hell. We have to get serious about evangelism. Wake up to what Christ has called His disciples to do! Souls will either go to Heaven or Hell. If we as followers of Christ are silent then many will go to Hell. Are you glad someone told you the truth? I am sure you are extremely glad that someone followed Christ's command by sharing the Gospel with you. Now let us follow Him and tell others, they will be glad that you did. The eternity of souls is in the balance of our choice to either disobey or obey Christ's clear call to follow Him no matter the cost.

Adila was a twelve-year-old, tender-hearted, bright, inquisitive girl. She had grown up in a devout Muslim home. Every Friday her family attended the local mosque where they had congregational prayer. Muslim men were required to attend, but it was optional for the women. Nonetheless, Adila had not missed one meeting her entire life and she was determined not to miss one now. As was her regular Friday routine, she walked in with her head covered and silently began praying in sacred awe and reverence to Allah. Growing up, she had been taught that she was named after Allah's most commonly referred to attributes.

Adila means "justice." It is one of the most vitally important characteristics of Allah. She was taught from an early age that Allah is a righteous judge that has very little patience for sin. She, along with the majority of the Islamic faith, have a skewed perspective of God. They see God as a hateful, condemning, monarch who rules with sovereignty and is waiting to destroy any who dare to transgress his commandments. As a result of looking at their god in this way, they have a false fear of him. Instead of being motivated by the love of a forgiving Father, they seek to please Allah because they fear that if they do not then he will utterly destroy them in the afterlife. As she was praying, Adila had many thoughts come to mind about the mysterious god she was told to reverence with the highest of esteem and obey without the slightest hesitation. She began to question every part of her faith in Allah. She questioned her beliefs, religious education, and the very foundations of her faith. She slowly began to realize that Allah is a loveless god who cares little about those who serve him. This moment initiated the embark of a lifelong journey to know the God that created her heart. She had a few secret Christian friends that she had kept hidden from her family, and she was continually drawn to the evident love that was freely shown by them. Adlia began studying the Bible at school in her free time. All while she continued the traditional motions of the lifeless religion of her family. She became infatuated with the God of the Bible. He was a righteous judge that condemns sin, but He was oh so much more than that! The God of the Bible loved Adila with an unconditional love and longed to forgive and forget her sins. What she would soon discover would completely alter life as she knew it. After several years of secretly learning more about this indescribable God, at age 17, she finally decided that Christ was far too good to keep to herself any longer. She boldly told her family that she had repented of her sins and received the gift of salvation through Jesus Christ. She knew the cost of telling them she had become a follower of Christ would be disappointment, discouragement, and utter amazement.

Knowing the price of what she was about to do, she unashamedly urged her family to turn from their sins and place complete trust in Christ alone. As she boldly proclaimed the Gospel of Jesus Christ, she felt a peace, comfort, and joy come over her like nothing she had ever experienced before. Her family, absolutely appalled at this news, started screaming at her and telling her that she was making a bad choice. They pleaded with her for about an hour to reconsider, but it was no use. Adila had encountered the Jesus of the Bible, and although she was unsure exactly where it would lead her, she was determined to follow Christ-no matter the cost.

The price Adila paid for choosing to follow Jesus that night was one of epic proportions. Her family, the same family she had grown up with all of the years previous, surrounded her and began to kick, punch, and mock her. Adila, shocked that this was happening, crouched into a fetal position and, in fear and confusion, began to cry out to her new-found God of love. As she occasionally looked up, she watched as her little sister whose hair she had braided hundreds of times and stayed up countless late nights talking, was being pressured and manipulated into beating her older sister. She watched as her older brother, with arms she once found comfort in when he fearlessly fought to protect her from guys, now relentlessly striking the same body he had previously protected. With tears in her eyes, bruises on her body, and brokenness in her heart, she was thrown outside of her house by her own parents. The same parents who kissed her goodnight, the same parents who told her they loved her, the same parents who raised her in hopes that she would follow in their footsteps, were now staring with scorn and disapproval in their eyes- Just how she had imagined her ex-god doing when she failed. Adila was truly heartbroken. She had been forsaken, beaten, mocked, abandoned, and disowned by the people she loved most. Wounded both physically and emotionally, she stumbled to her feet and began walking to the closest Bible preaching church she knew. When she arrived, she was embraced by the custodians and leaders of the church. They began to comfort with Jesus' words, "Blessed are they which are persecuted for righteousness' sake: for theirs is the kingdom of Heaven. Blessed are ye when men shall revile you, and persecute you, and shall say all manner of evil against you falsely for my sake. Rejoice, and be exceeding glad: for great is your reward in Heaven: for so persecuted the prophets which were before you."[7] They went on to explain that what she did was very brave and is what Jesus told us would happen if we were to truly abandon all and follow Him.

The following Sunday morning, Adila gave her testimony of how she decided to follow Jesus. As she began describing that painful night, tears streamed down her cheeks and formed a small puddle on the podium. There was a dead silence in the auditorium as the congregation was imagining what she went through. This was sacrifice. This was surrender. Adila experienced what it truly means to forsake all and follow Christ. She forsook her family. She forsook her comfort. She forsook her religion. She forsook stability. She forsook the conditional love of her biological family. She forsook herself completely. Why? Because Jesus was (and still is) worth abandoning everything for, and her story shows what it really means to follow Christ.

How about you? Is Jesus Christ worth total abandonment to you? Have you seen in Christ something worth surrendering earthly comfort for? Is the Savior worth relinquishing the temporary pleasures of sin? To what extent are you willing to deny your will, your comforts, your desires, your ambitions, and your life for Christ?

The Bible speaks of a certain man had the boldness to tell Jesus that he would follow Him anywhere that He went.[8] Now, in most people's minds, we see a seemingly committed potential follower of Christ who is willing to follow Him anywhere. However, Jesus saw something far deeper than the words that he spoke- Jesus saw the man's heart. He knew that this potential follower wanted to follow Him only out of his selfish ambitions. As a result of this man's reaction to Christ's response to His seemingly selfless statement, we can conclude that he was only interested in following Christ for what he could eventually receive from the long awaited King of the world. To price of following Christ was exponentially higher than he originally anticipated. In his mind, following Jesus meant much like it means for many proclaimed Christians today.

This man figured that by following Jesus he would get to stay in what would be known as a presidential suite today. He wanted to enjoy all of the luxuries that he, like the majority of the Jewish people, believed Jesus would incur as earthly king. He expected reward for his loyalty. He expected to live in extravagant housing, eat delicious food, and experience the excessively elaborate lifestyle of royalty. He wanted to participate in the future pleasures of being a friend of the future King at the expense of little commitment. Many times, if we are completely honest with ourselves, we do the same thing. We can often be guilty of pursuing Christ for what He can do for us instead of following Him out of our love for what He has done for us.

This certain man was an investor. He wanted to invest his loyalty in hopes that his investment would eventually pay out in abundance. Little to his surprise, this King had a different agenda than most imagined. Christ was indeed the king, but not in the way that this investor expected. After hearing the Messiah's response, he was simply unwilling to invest his time, energy, and life into someone with so little to offer physically but asked so much in return. He perceived that following Jesus everywhere meant living the "high life," when in reality, following Jesus meant living the "low life." The cost of following Christ is still the same today.

The prosperity gospel is a deceptive religious belief teaching that God always wants to boost one's income and physical well-being as long as that person is faithful, positive, and generous to a certain church or charitable organization. Unlike the preaching of the prosperity gospel, in most cases, you will not experience an exponential rise in your monetary gain, but rather be encouraged to give more for the advancement of Christ's Kingdom. You are not automatically guaranteed to be immune to every sickness and disease, but God could choose to put you through a difficult trial like that to weaken you so that you rely even more on His strength. When you surrender all to Christ and follow Him, you will not experience many the pleasures this world has to offer because you will discover that the only place that provides true, everlasting joy and satisfaction is found in the risen Son of the Living God.

At this point, having seen first-hand what true abandonment of self and true reliance of Christ looks like, you and I have a decision to make. We can either decide to remain wallowing in the filth of this world's fleeting pleasures, or decide to recklessly abandon all of our sinful desires in return for knowing God deeper and experiencing all that He has to offer His children. There is no in-between. There is no middle ground. We can no longer stand idly and take part in the "best of both worlds" scenario. We cannot continue to have one foot in the rebellious wickedness of the world, and be one with Christ and enjoy the confidence of knowing that we are one of God's children. Take a moment to look deep down inside your soul and evaluate the true reason behind why you are following Jesus.

What is God's Will for My Life?

This question, "What is God's will for my life?" is perhaps one of the most pondered questions among Christians today. We are forced to make decisions every day. Many times the driving force behind each decision is a tough situation. Do we always seek God's will when we make a decision, even if the decision is small? Some choices we make seem less important, so how do we learn to follow God's will even with the small decision? What should I wear today? Is my gas tank really on empty or will I be able to get to work and back without breaking down? What should I eat today? Should I cook my own food or eat out? If I eat out where should I go? How should I respond to this annoying bus kid at church? Can I make it through this yellow light or should I play it safe and slow down?

Other decisions carry much more weight and are of far greater significance. Should I go to college? If so, where should I go? What do I want to be doing for the rest of my life? Should I date? If so, who should date? When should I plan on getting married? Should we have kids? If so, how many kids should we have? Where should we put them in school: Public, Private, or homeschool?

Perhaps William Carey conveys it best when he said, "To know the will of God, we need only an open Bible and an open map".

Together we will discover God's will and learn to live in obedience to it. Stop treating God like the Easter bunny. God is not hiding His will from us. He never told us to find His will, yet many times that is exactly what we do. Perhaps you can relate the following scenario, "Alright kids we are going to have an Easter egg hunt. All of you stay inside until the Easter bunny gets done hiding the eggs all over the neighborhood and then he will let you know when you can come out and find them. Only this time he has put each of your names in an egg. Find your egg and bring it to him and he will give you twenty dollars." Although this is not what is really going on, it seems to be similar to what we imagine God and His will to be. Many questions arise in our minds and we inquire of the Lord to reveal His will as if he was withholding it from us. The will of God was never intended to be found, but followed. God has freely revealed His will to us in His inherent Word.

God is not a monarchical ruler who desires for his subjects to live in darkness constantly wondering what next steps to take. God wants to make His will known to us. In the following paragraphs, we will discuss several verses where God quite clearly makes known His will to us.

God's Will is that We Give Thanks In all Things

> "In every thing give thanks: for this is the will of God in Christ Jesus concerning you." 1 Thessalonians 5:18

God wills for followers of Christ to be thankful in all things. He desires that we show appreciation to Him and others. God has done amazing things for us. He has preserved my life far longer than I deserve and without Him there is no telling where I would be today. I can recall only a mere 100 times where I had a "saw my life flash before my eyes" moment. But there are doubtless thousands of times that God preserved our lives and we had no knowledge of it. I can remember one such time vividly.

It was a hot summer day in mid-July as I rushed to finish the many yards I had scheduled to cut for the day. I stopped by my house for some cold iced water to quench my thirsting body that refused to go on without refreshment. I guzzled down two or three cups and hurriedly ran out the door. In my fast-paced determination to finish all the work I left one essential item inside the house, my truck keys. I quickly went back into the house and grabbed them. I was so busy that I did not even stop to ask God for a safe and productive day. While I was driving God woke me up to a startling reality. As I drove down that familiar road on this typical summer afternoon I suddenly witnessed a violent and horrific crash. A two ton tractor trailer collided head-on with a minivan at an intersection. I was immediately filled with fear and dread for both of the parties involved in this gut-wrenching scene. I instantly called the police and told them what happened. The driver that caused the wreck was drunk. After hearing my testimony of what happened, they told me to leave as they informed me that I would not want to see them drag the lifeless bodies out of the van.

I left the scene of the accident in shock. I was breathlessly amazed that God would allow something like that to happen. It was just at the moment when I was beginning to become confused and angry at how the Father could willingly allow such a thing to happen that it was almost as if I heard the words "it could have been you." I pulled over and was overwhelmed at the realization of my selfish and ungrateful attitude towards God. I was treating God, the One who gave His only Son for me, as unjust. Who was I to question my God? He is the Creator of all the universe and holds everything in His hands, and I had the audacity to question Him? I felt ashamed at my thoughts. I began pondering how many near-death experiences I had been through that I had never realized. I should not be alive. You should not be alive. The fact that we are alive is proof that God is not finished with us yet. He wants us to look to Him alone as the sole source of our thanks. God's will is that you and I constantly remain in an attitude of gratitude and live lives reflecting that we are forgiven. Every breath we take is a reminder that we are here for a reason: to know Christ deeper so that we will make Christ known more effectively.

God's Will is that We Abstain from Sexual Sin

> "For this is the will of God, even your sanctification, that ye should abstain from fornication:" 1 Thessalonians 4:3

According to this verse, it is God's will that we "abstain from fornication" or sexual sin. God only uses pure vessels. His will is for us to remain pure. No matter how impossible this may seem to be in our sex-crazed society, God expects and demands that we live holy and pure lives. We cannot do this in and of ourselves, but through Jesus Christ it is possible. We must constantly rely on Christ and His righteousness to sanctify us if we truly want to live pure and holy lives. This does not mean we will never fail- we certainly will fail at times. However, it does mean that when we do fail, we confess our sin and repent of our unrighteousness. When we truly repent (or turn away from) our sin, Christ automatically imputes His righteousness to us. (Read Romans 4:20-25) In this passage of Romans, it is evident that righteousness was imputed unto Abraham for his faith. Look closely at verses 23-25, in these verses we learn that righteousness was not imputed to Abraham alone, but also to everyone that believes that Jesus Christ died and rose again. Please, do not miss this incredible truth, you and I can be righteous through Christ's righteousness! Now that we are righteous, God wants us to remain in a state of purity. God specifically mentions to evade sexual sin for a reason. When we cross God's boundaries there are always detrimental consequences as a result. God tells us it is His will for us to avoid all sexual activity outside the bounds of marriage. This is not because He wants us to be miserable or to imprison us from the world's idea of "fun". The truth is the Father wants us to seek our fulfillment in Him alone because He knows that we will only have true joy when we find our satisfaction in Him alone. We will discover infinitely more peace and contentment in Christ than we will by indulging in the temporary pleasure of sin. When we seek to please God and are willing to follow His will then we gain true joy and satisfaction that cannot be found inside the world.

God's Will is that We Are Actively Involved in Global Evangelism

> "The Lord is not slack concerning his promise, as some men count slackness; but is longsuffering to us-ward, not willing that any should perish, but that all should come to repentance." 2 Peter 3:9

God's will is that no one should go to Hell- a place that He originally created for the devil and his demons. God's will is that everyone in the world repents of their futile attempts to find peace, satisfaction, and joy in sin. God's will is that the world would be saved. The One who spoke the universe into being is far more than capable of forcing His will upon everyone, but He chooses to give us a free will. He chooses to use people that have experienced His love as tools to reach people who have never experienced His love. God wants to use you to get the gospel to the world. We, who were once lost and are now found are called to tell the lost how they can be found. We, who were once dead in our trespasses and sins and are now alive in Christ, are commanded to bring the dead to the Life-Giver.

It only makes since to share good news with others. I mean, how selfish and heartless would it be if someone discovered the effectively efficient cure to cancer, aids, and ALS, yet chose to keep it to themselves? How much more absurd would it be if someone knew the cure to sin, death, and hell, yet chose to willingly withhold the cure from all those who are infected? Physical diseases are horrifying. Each of us has gone through the pain of losing or knowing someone who has lost a loved one to a deadly disease. Disease is a direct result of humanity's choice to sin. Physical death is truly awful. There is a disease that is far more painful than any sickness could even compare to, and that is sin. There is a second death that is far worse than the first death. Hell is real. Ever sinner will go to Hell. We, who have received the cure, must tell the sick about the Savior. It is the duty of every saint to share the gospel with every sinner.

God's will; giving thanks to the Lord, abstaining from sexual sins, and contributing to global evangelism, these are essential ways that a Christian continually lives in God's will. Today followers of Christ need to take a stand and obey. God's will is clear, but many times we do not put in the time and effort to even learn God's will. In Psalms, the psalmist yearns for God saying "Teach me to do thy will. . ."[9] God's will is not always easy to follow, but God will help us. When we seek to follow the Lord and pour His Word into our lives then we will discover that the price of following Christ is truly insignificant in light of all that He has done for us.

Answering the Tough Questions

Why would a good God allow bad things to happen to good people? The truth is that good people do not exist. Jesus tells us that none are good but God alone.[10] Jesus Christ was the only good person to have ever lived. Although we may describe certain people as "good," there is nothing "good" about them. We deserve Hell. This is a difficult truth for us to swallow, but it is the truth nevertheless and the sooner we realize it the better. God allows things to happen to certain people for reasons that we do not understand. We cannot possibly fathom God's nature and actions. This is a good thing as it forces us to have faith. As we faithfully trust the Father, He will cause everything that we go through to result in our good and His glory.

Job was a man who perfectly illustrates the idea of faithful trust in the Father in order to give Him glory. He is described in the Bible as a man who "was perfect and upright, and one that feared God, and eschewed evil."[11] Job feared the Lord. Job was rewarded for fearing the Lord. He "was the greatest man in all of the east."[12] Later we see that God blessed Job with seven sons and three daughters. Job made sacrifices on the behalf of His family. God thought highly of Job. In fact, God thought so highly of Job that He bragged about Him. I do not know about you, but it feels really good to be bragged on. Whether it is a parent, teacher, coach, pastor, boss, or even a friend, when others think enough about you to tell others how awesome you are, it makes you feel wonderful. Imagine how it must have felt to be held in high regard by the very One who breathed the world into existence.

The following narrative is a paraphrase by the author. There was a day when the sons of God presented themselves before the Lord. As the beautiful angels humbly bowed in awe before their Creator, so likewise did the exquisite, outlawed accuser of the brethren. To whom the Potentate One asked, "Where did you come from?" The deceiver answered, "From walking up and down in the earth." Then the Lord said unto Satan, "Have you considered my servant Job, that there is none like him in all the earth? He is a perfect and upright man that fears God and departs from evil." (What a testimony!) The Devil responds, "Of course he fears you, you've protected him, his family, and all that he has. You have blessed him with substance and he is considered the greatest man in the east! If you take away his blessings he will curse you to your face!" Then the Lord did something that Job and all that knew him would not understand. The Sovereign One gave limited power to the adversary. He was going to test Job to see just how much he truly loved Him. God is omnipotent. Meaning He knows and understands all things. He saw the end for Job. He knew Job would be in pain. He foresaw Job's confusion and doubt in the loving God he thought he knew and trusted. He knew Job would not understand, but that, despite all the odds, he would endure till the end and sin not with his mouth. He knew that in the end Job would be blessed more than he was in the beginning.

Our understanding, like Job's, is finite. We cannot see the end result like God does. The Lord thinks and acts differently than we do. His thoughts are not our thoughts. His ways are not our ways.[13] If we knew the exact intent of God's actions and their results that we would not need faith. The Lord wants us to trust Him. When we cannot trace God's hand, we must trust His plan. The Lord is trustworthy and deserving of our lives. He has never failed and He never will.

While God desired for Job to see that He alone is in complete control and for Job's love to grow stronger, Job did not initially understand... He was doing so well that God himself bragged on him. I do not believe that God "punishes" His children. Job was doing everything right by fearing God, hating evil, and following God, yet Job most likely felt he was being punished. When we choose to disobey Him by transgressing His commandments, we will reap the consequences of those choices. God has given us the choice to either sow unto righteousness and reap unto everlasting peace, life and Heaven or sow unto sin and reap everlasting destruction, death, and hell. The choice is ours. While God does not provide pain, despair, and trials, He is not limited by them. God can use pain, despair, and trials to accomplish His will by allowing us to see that He is in control of all and He is enough for us.

God is perfect in all of His ways. He makes no mistakes. Has it ever occurred to you that nothing has ever occurred to God? Look at the story of Samson found in Judges 14 for example. He was a judge of God who decided to do his own thing in his own way. The story of Samson is proof that anyone can be used of God. Samson was an adulterous womanizer which eventually resulted in him being blinded and humiliated in front of the Philistines. Even though Samson suffered much embarrassment and discomfort due to his poor choices, God was not limited by his sin. God allowed Samson's hair to grow and strength to return while he was in captivity. The Philistines called Samson to come out so they could mock him and they put him between two pillars of a house. There were 3,000 people on the roof alone. Samson then prayed to God to strengthen him for the last time so that he could be avenged of the Philistines for blinding his eyes. The Lord granted him strength and Samson took hold of the pillars and the entire house collapsed killing him as well as all of the people present. The Bible says, "So the dead that he killed in his death were more than those whom he killed in his life."[14]

God accomplished His permissive will in Samson regardless of his rebellion to His perfect will. God will use who He chooses to accomplish what He wants whether we agree to do what He says or not. God is not the One limited by sin, we are. Those who choose to do things contrary to how God instructs, will reap the results of their choices, but are not a stumbling block to the Limitless One. God wants to use us to accomplish His perfect will in us, but we must be willing to live in active obedience to His commands in order to experience the joyfully abundant life that Christ promises.

Jacob and Rachel's firstborn son was named Joseph. He was highly esteemed both in the eyes of his earthly father and his Heavenly Father. In the same way that Jacob loved Rachel more than Leah, Jacob favored Joseph above all of his other children. In fact, Jacob favored Joseph so much, that he gave Joseph a coat of many colors. The coat would have been a very costly gift, clearly distinguishing Joseph above his less loved brothers. This automatically made him despised in his brothers' eyes. Soon jealousy was sparked in the hearts of all his brothers.

Joseph told his brothers a dream. In his dream, he and his brothers were both gathering sheaves of wheat when all of the sudden, his sheave stood up and all the sheaves of his brothers were obedient to his sheave. As you could imagine, this made his brothers even madder at him than before! Joseph then decided to tell his family a second dream. This time the sun, moon, and eleven stars worshiped him. Now when his father, whom loved him dearly, heard this dream, he rebuked him and asked if he and his mother should also bow down to the earth in reverence to him. At this point his brothers envied him greatly. The jealously that began small, soon grew until it became hatred. Eventually this hate turned to wrath as his brothers conspired his demise.

One day, his brothers went to feed their father's flock in another city. Jacob called for Joseph who was eager and willing to obey his father's requests. The mission Jacob had for his beloved son was to go and check on his brothers and the flock and return again safely to him. Off Joseph went in humble obedience to his father's will, and by so doing, he was in the center of God's will. As he approached his brothers, they began to conspire against his life. Then they would simply lie to their father and tell them some beast had eaten him. At the expense of Joseph's life, their problem would be solved. The eldest son, Reuben, was against killing Joseph therefore he recommended that they simply toss Joseph in a pit for a short amount of time. His brothers were content with this conclusion and threw him into the pit. Reuben purposed to return later and deliver him back to his father.

As some of the brothers were eating bread, a caravan was passing through on their way to sell in Egypt. So when Judah heard it, he thought it would be a clever idea to sell Joseph as a slave. Judah though it was a win-win situation, they could get some extra money and Joseph could live. All of the brothers present agreed and they sold Joseph. When Reuben returned, who apparently was unaware of the transaction, he found the pit empty. Joseph was gone. Reuben was very upset at his brothers, but he, along with his brothers, decided to conceal the truth from their father. The brothers then went and killed a baby goat and dipped Joseph's coat in blood and brought it to their father asking him if it belonged to his beloved son. Jacob was truly heartbroken as he thought a wild animal had viciously devoured him.

So far, Joseph has had it pretty rough. He told his brothers his dreams and they hated him with pure jealousy. All of the sudden, he is being fought over what should be done to him. Finally, he catches a break. He gets to live, but as a slave. But the Lord was not finished with Joseph. Joseph continually sought the Lord and lived his life in obedience to God's will. God blessed Joseph and caused him to be a prosperous man. Now when his master, Potiphar, saw that the Lord made all that Joseph did to prosper, he made him the overseer over his house and put him in charge of all his possessions. God's Word teaches us that not only Potiphar, but his entire house and fields were abundantly blessed of the Lord because of Joseph. Joseph had the highest position that can be obtained as a slave. It was as if he was second in command of the secret services for Pharaoh. Potiphar gave him his bank card and told him what to get, where to go, and what to do. Unknown to him, God's plan for Joseph was to prosper and give him a position that was far beyond what Joseph could have ever possibly imagined.

That is the way that God works. He loves us. He wants to do more in and through us than we could ever imagine possible! But Joseph was not yet ready for the great position that God had in store for him. He still lacked the patience, humility, and wisdom that would be required to rule second-in-command of the greatest kingdom of earth, Egypt. In order to see how faithful Joseph was to the Lord, he had to first be tested. This test came in the form of his master's wife. She tempted him on a daily basis to have an affair with her. To which he responded, "How can I do this great wickedness and sin against God?"[15] Joseph kept refusing her sinful request repeatedly. One day, as Joseph was going about his normal business, Potiphar's wife caught him by his garment and begged him to commit sin with her. Joseph left his garment and fled out of the house. He obeyed the Lord by fleeing from sin. Joseph had successfully passed the test.

Little did he know, this was only the beginning of many more trials to come. As you could imagine, the adulterous hearted woman was not happy to say the least. When Potiphar came home later that day, she falsely accused Joseph of attempting to rape her. The evidence of his crime was in her hands, Joseph's garments. What other proof did Potiphar need? Joseph had been framed. His master was furious. He took Joseph and cast him into the prison. Imagine with me what Joseph might have been thinking. He obeyed the Lord and this is how he gets rewarded for it. Joseph had every reason to give up on God, but though all the trouble Joseph only grew stronger in his faith. Think about all the troubles of Joseph: his brothers abandoned him and sold him into slavery, his master's wife tempted him with sin where he overcame the temptation, and now his master has sentenced him to prison for a crime he did not commit. Think about the application, would you continue to obey God if this were your circumstances?

We find that the Lord was with Joseph and showed him mercy by allowing him to find favor with the keeper of the prison.[16] Immediately after the guy who was in charge of the prisoners encountered Joseph, he gave all the prisoners into the care of Joseph and never worried about him again because the Lord made everything that he did to prosper. Wow! Those who desire to be prosperous ought to take notes from Joseph. Joseph had it going on. No matter where he was or what he was doing, he was prosperous! One day Pharaoh became angry at the men who prepared his food and drink. He had both of these men thrown into the same prison as Joseph. One night both men had a dream. When Joseph came to check on them in the morning, they were sad because no one could interpret their strange dreams. Then Joseph, giving glory in advance to the One who will one day receive all glory, made it clear that interpretations come from God Almighty. Notice that Joseph was careful to give God glory and did not attempt to take any credit for anything he did. If we are to be prosperous, we must do the same.

They both had strange dreams and God gave Joseph the interpretation of them. Servants of God are called to serve others. God will always aid His followers as they aim to help others. The exact interpretation God gave him came to pass. At Pharaoh's feast, he beheaded the baker and restored the butler to his position. Although the butler promised to remember Joseph once he got out, he thought only of himself and his thoughts of Joseph escaped his mind. Eventually the Pharaoh himself had a dream that no one could interpret. Immediately the butler remembered how Joseph provided an accurate interpretation of his dream and told Pharaoh. Pharaoh summoned this supposed "dream interpreter" and the Lord made known the dream to Joseph. When Pharaoh heard thereof, he was shocked and amazed Pharaoh made Joseph second in command of all in the greatest empire at the time. God always richly blesses those who are willing to patiently wait and completely trust in Him alone. God used Joseph as an instrument to make known His riches abundantly to the world. God gave prestige to Joseph whose sole desire was to give glory to God. The Bible says, "Humble yourselves under the mighty hand of God that He may exalt thee in due time."[17] It is God that exalts. The person who attempts to temporarily exalt themselves will be humbled by the Exalter. God lifted Joseph up to a position of honor and respect only after he had learned to honor and respect God. God will only exalt those who humble themselves to the extent that they only desire His exaltation.

Challenge

What can we learn from this passage in God's Word? How can we take the truths we find in this passage and apply them to our life? I am not sure who you are or what you have gone through, but odds are, you have gone through difficult times in your past. You can rest assured that God never puts you through more than you can endure.[18] Everything God allows to happen, He does for a reason. If you are still breathing, God has delivered you from past trials and He is capable of bringing you through current and future storms in this life.

Chapter 9

Persecution: Why Do We Have so Little of What Christ Promised so Much of?

Let me tell you a story about a boy named Quingling. His name means: "celebration of understanding" (This will be an important detail to remember later on). Quingling lives in Japan. His entire upbringing of 18 years has been engrossed in the atheistic culture and society of his country. His family has raised him with the idea that perfection is the only option and anything short of it is utter failure. He has excelled to the top of his class in school and is on track to attend the most esteemed university in the country. So far, He has made his family proud. He has achieved academic success and completed every task his parents have given him with utmost excellence. One day his family throws a party for Quingling's success in his schooling. His family invites as many friends and neighbors as can fit into the house and his proud parents boast about how the meaning of their son's name matches his position in society. Beaming with pride and joy, they exclaim "Quingling has lived up to his name this day." Quingling has "arrived" in the eyes of most people in Japan. But Quingling is not happy. Deep down inside he knows there is something missing from his life. He longs to ease the deep desperation of his heart and soul. At the party Quingling met a girl named Areum. This girl was different than any other girl he has ever met. He is fascinated with her peculiar mannerisms and personality. Areum talks much differently than most people. She told Quingling of a God that she has encountered that has radically transformed her life from pointless and dead to purposeful and alive! She talks with such passion and excitement that Quingling was instantly intrigued and inquired to know more about the life-changing deity of his new friend. After briefly exchanging phone numbers, they both went their separate ways.

Over the next few weeks, Quingling, tortured by interest in Areum's God, began communicating continually with Areum. He asked question after question about God in his hopes to discover the same joy and purposefulness as Areum. One day, after multiple invitations, Quingling decided to attend a small secret church that met at 2 in the morning deep inside a basement. This was a very different setting than the places where Quingling spent most of his time. As he stared in amazement at these believers, he was amazed at their faith. Men, women, boys, and girls huddled together in close circles where they thanked God for giving them the opportunity to read the few dilapidated pages of scripture that had been smuggled in by fearless missionaries, who had brought them at the cost of their own lives. They cried out praises to a God that Quingling could not physically see. He wondered how these followers of Christ could devote themselves to this God. At that meeting Quingling heard the gospel. He heard that God did, in fact, exist and that He, unlike his parents, did not expect perfection. He heard that he had sinned against God and deserved to go to an awful place called Hell. This news convicted Quingling deeply. Although he knew he should repent of his sin and choose to follow Christ, he feared disappointing his parents and letting his family down. After all, achieving academic excellence in order to get a high paying job and make his family proud had been his entire purpose for living. This newly discovered God made Quingling rethink the entire reason he was living. He kept returning to this secret meeting whenever they convened. The more he learned about this loving God, the more fascinated and hungry he became to know more. One night, after struggling for many months with the choice to abandon everything for Christ, Quingling decided to follow Jesus. He knew it would cost him much, but he did not yet know that it would cost him his very life. But Quingling had decided that no matter the cost, he would follow Christ. He prayed a simple prayer in his heart and realized it was not merely a prayer that saved him, but the amazing grace of God. That same night, Quingling was filled with uncontainable joy! He excitedly told his family about his decision to follow the Savior. His family disowned him. His mother said that she wished he had never been born. His father said that he was no longer his son. They told him to leave and to never return. Quingling expected a less than enthusiastic response, but this was too much to bear. He went to the underground church and told the pastor what his decision to follow Christ cost him. The pastor showed him Matthew 5:10-12 and told him that such persecution is a sign that he was being obedient to Christ. Quingling became a completely changed man. He went around boldly sharing the gospel with friends and even strangers. Many came and a handful of them decided to follow Jesus. The Lord was using Quingling in amazing ways. He invited his family to the secret meeting. To his surprise, both his mother and father came to the meeting. Soon afterwards, they reported the secret church meeting to the authorities. One night during a worship service the police raided the church. They took Quingling and the other believers to jail for questioning. After severely beating them, the police reluctantly released them with a warning that if they were caught assembling again then they would endure far worse treatment. Little did the police know, but Quingling and his fellow believers had given their lives completely to Christ to the extent that they could say with confidence "Christ is my life." Can you truly say with complete assurance that Christ is your life?

Quingling and his fellow believers in Christ abandoned everything for Jesus. The following night, knowing the cost, the small group of believers moved locations to worship their Lord. They talked about the fact that continuing to meet in fellowship could very well cost them their lives. Each of the believers spoke up about how, although they knew the cost, they were willing to die in order to obey the Word of God. Three nights later the police found the place they were meeting and raided the location as these believers were singing the song "I have decided to follow Jesus." The policemen cut off the electricity and stormed the building. The sign of the nearly twenty heavily armed policemen caused the believers to immediately go silent. The policemen started yelling for everyone to get on their knees and denounce that Jesus was the Son of God. They threatened to kill the family members of each believer. They threatened to shoot each of them that did not renounce Christ. After minutes of intense pressure to deny their Savior, an elderly lady began to quietly sing the chorus of the song the entire group had been singing before the police entered the room. She began singing "I have decided to follow Jesus; I have decided to follow Jesus; No turning back; No turning back." The guards were in awe. They began screaming at her to stop singing, but their shouting was soon drowned out by the voices of the believers who had now joined in singing with her. The believers sang together "The world behind me, the cross before me; No turning back, no turning back." What started out as a quiet song soon turned into a bold melody of words that penetrated through the walls. The spirit of the Living God was present in the room and arrested the hearts of those who came with the intention of arresting the believers. Every officer dropped his gun, began weeping, and after several minutes, joined the believers in singing. Everyone within the walls of the building were now singing "Though none go with me, still I will follow; No turning back, no turning back." They eagerly asked the pastor to tell them more about this Jesus of whom the believers clearly knew. The pastor, still shaking from nervousness, opened the few pages of scripture he had and preached the gospel to them. Each officer chose to follow Christ even though they knew it meant abandoning their occupation and would completely alter their lives as they knew it. Every believer in the room would later be tortured and killed for their faith in Christ. As a result of their commitment to Christ, many souls would come to a saving knowledge of Christ.

How Have We been Persecuted?

People like Quingling, Areum, and the police officers literally gave up everything for the cause of Christ. What have we given up for Christ? How have we been persecuted? In what ways have we suffered for Christ's sake? If we are honest, most of us have sacrificed very little in comparison to what fellow believers around the world have sacrificed. I mean, who do you know personally that has suffered considerable persecution as a result of preaching the gospel or living it out?

Growing up, I can remember feeling proud of the fact that I had been cussed out and rejected by certain individuals. I thought to myself, "I am being persecuted for Christ's sake. This is awesome! I must be doing something right." Although I was enduring a form of persecution, it was quite insignificant in comparison to how much others around the world have suffered.

In our Americanized Christian society, we have so little of the great things that Christ promised to his followers. Why is this the case? Is it because we have been deceived into believing that every American has been saved and is on their way to Heaven? Certainly not. I clearly remember sitting in a barber shop when I struck up a conversation with the 3 men sitting beside and across from me. I handed each of them a gospel tract and they asked me why I am willing to boldly share my faith with strangers. I responded by saying "I was once diagnosed with a life-threatening illness. I was born with an awful disease and there was nothing I or any doctor could ever do to cure me. The only way I could be saved was if Someone else chose to die so that I could live. I was hopeless. One day, I learned that Someone willingly gave His life so that I could have life through Him." I then explained to them that the terminal disease I had was sin and the One who gave His life to save me was Jesus Christ. Each of them told me they had never once heard the message that Christ had died to save them and rose again to give them life through Him. One man told me that I was a fool and mocked me for a few minutes. The other told me that it was too good to be true and I should not go around spreading lies. One man asked me to pray with him about his salvation. I gave them all a card with my phone number so they could contact me with further questions. I left that afternoon with more than a new haircut, I left with an entirely different perspective. I realized that there really were people even in America who had never once heard a clear presentation of the gospel.

Revival is a Result of Persecution

Various statistics show that only 39 percent of professed Christians in America have shared the gospel within the last 6 months. It is no wonder that churches are shriveling up and dying all across the United States. Christians pray for revival, but revival is a direct result of obedience to Christ. If we would actually do in faith what Christ has commanded us to do, revival would soon follow. Would you be included in the 39 percent who actively share the gospel with others? If so, you know that persecution is a direct result of obedience to Christ.

Whenever someone is willing to stand up against sin they will be met with sharp confrontation. Persecution should be expected by every true follower of Christ. True revival is the fruit of severe persecution. We can look to the infamous 9/11 attack as an example of this. As horrendously terrible as the attack was, the results of it happening are truly astounding. Some estimates say that nearly half of the adult population attended a church service on the weekend following the heart-wrenching attacks. An exponential amount of spiritual concern took place on the weeks just after 9/11 as Americans took notice of just how brief life is and evaluated what really matters most. Many churches experienced a doubled attendance rate on the weeks following an attack on U.S. soil. Although the majority of people never returned again, this brief growth in revival resulted immediately after persecution on our country. The exact same results were found after the attack on Pearl Harbor.

Persecution always results in a turn of people's hearts to God. Will it take another catastrophic event such as 9/11 or Pearl Harbor to turn the hearts of Americans back to the One it was founded upon? I certainly hope not.

In scripture we see examples where persecution was used to spread the gospel all throughout the known world. When the church in Jerusalem underwent severe persecution Christians were forced to flee from the city to various cities around it. When Saul and other persecutors began persecuting them in those cities they fled to, they began running to more cities until the entire country and other countries heard of Christ who they preached when they fled.[1]

How Would You Respond to Persecution?

The following story is a true account of a violent act that happened in within a public school in America.

It was a routine Thursday morning at a local community college in the western United States, when an armed student charged into classrooms. This gunman was serious and on a mission of harm. A witness later described that the gunman seemed to be singling out Christians. According to the accounts of multiple eyewitnesses, the gunman told everyone in the room that if they stood up identifying themselves as Christians then he was going to shoot them in the head, but if they did not stand he would only shoot them in the leg. The shooter then asked those who were unashamed of Christ to take a stand for Him in death. Nine students stood up. He shot each one of them in the head instantly ending their lives. After shooting everyone else in the leg, the gunman shot himself ending his life. This is truly a sobering story that happened in America. There have been multiple other occasions where Christians have been targeted specifically and asked if they would be willing to die for choosing to follow Christ. I am not trying to scare you, but these types of things really have happened and will mostly likely happen again. I want you to determine how you would respond in one of these situations. Do you have such a deep and personal relationship with Christ that you would be willing to die for Him today? Jesus Christ calls us to deny ourselves and to follow Him even in death.

Forgiveness > Judgement

"Master, come and eat! The food is ready." Simon had asked the Messiah to come and eat with him and some friends at the synagogue. Surely this would be a perfect time to understand the reason behind Jesus' teachings and find a way to prevent Him from continuing to teach. Perhaps this could even shift Jesus' focus and compromise His work this evening. Was he a prophet like many were saying? Simon was thoughtfully determined to find out.

As Jesus politely obliged his host and sat down, there was a knock at the door and the servant moves hastily to open it. Everyone in the room was filled with surprise to see the well-known harlot of the city at the door and entering the supper. She was carrying a small box in her hand and the people of the room, especially Simon, were both curious of the box and displeased at her presence. Her boldness at coming here had aroused such astonishment that no man in her view knew what to think or even say. Shaking, yet not seeming to notice her disruption, she approached the place where Jesus sat at the table from behind.

Jesus did not say a word, but He turned His head to see her face as she sank to the floor and removed the red ribbon from the box she held so close. Ever so carefully, she broke the box over His feet and used her hair to spread the ointment all over. In tearful reverence to Jesus, she bowed her head to kiss each foot with tenderness.

Simon, after gaining his composure, was thoroughly embarrassed. Irritably, he thought to himself, "If Jesus were a prophet, he would know what kind of woman it is who would dare to make her presence known here, let alone to touch him like that. She is a sinner!"

By this time also, some of the Pharisees in the room had recovered from the initial shock of this woman's presence and began whispering amongst themselves, criticizing her actions. They commented under their breath to each other saying, "Wasted."

Three Months Before

"Wasted"

I had heard this word on more than one occasion in my twenty some years. And as familiar as it was to me, I still felt the stinging impact of spite in the purposeful tone of its speaker strike me each time I heard it. Of course, by now, I had learned to disregard it, to in a way ignore its meaning as if I did not know the true nature of its implication. After all, its use in describing my life was mostly accurate. And I could hardly begin to find a reason to deny this unchangeable reality.

My mother died when I was twelve years old. She had been the last person in my life to ever make me feel anything but what this harsh reality had come to mean for me. My father had been a drunk for as long as I could remember and he took it upon himself to remind me every day after my mother's death I was her responsibility. He did not have time to care for her "mishap," as was his term for his my mere existence He treated me as if I was not his own flesh and blood, but I am.

When I turned thirteen, my father sold me to a foreign merchant in Jerusalem in exchange for money to buy more drinks. I will never forget that day. As I was being dragged away into an uncertain, terrifying future, I remember screaming at the top of my lungs for him to take me back. He scoffed at my humiliation and to further degrade me, repeated one word I would come to know all too well. "Wasted." And I never saw him again.

The merchant who had bought me for so little a price from my father was an Egyptian man who prided himself on finding rare beauties to auction off to the wealthiest bidder within Jerusalem's walls. I suffered the impending rage he used to fuel his beatings and endured much torment at the expense of his whip. After months of what he liked to refer to as "training," I was ready to be sold again, this time for much larger price.

When placed on the auction block for the first time at the age of fourteen and I could hardly bring myself to raise my head as the weight of shame I continually bore drowned me in a sea of hopelessness. My lack of appropriate clothing was enough to destroy any dignity I had left and the effort placed into making my body appear more attractive to the right buyer left me to feel like a tarnished being, depreciating with every touch and exploitation. I did not know my fate, but I knew the verity of my new forced identity. Not only did I recognize this, but it seemed as if every onlooker and passerby sensed it too. As if with casual banter, the sometimes mumbled but mostly bellowed response from their lips would be the same. "Wasted."

It did not take long for each master who purchased me to become quickly dissatisfied. I had so little to offer. Soon each master used me and passed me along like a piece of clothing that is only worn for a short amount and time and then discarded for something new. Time after time I was given at my master's discretion for the pleasing of business partners, friends, and relatives. I was even given to enemies as a payment for friendship. There was nothing my body had neither seen nor been through by the time I reached my early twenties.

Then one day it happened. My current owner had decided to sell me. Yet this deal was different than the others. My worth had reached a new low as my master finally convinced a buyer to purchase me at a price lower than what my father sold me for at the age of thirteen. I remember his disinterested look of disgust at seeing me for the first time, still he was convinced to buy me. The way he casually shrugged his shoulders as he handed over the payment let me know that he had little purpose for me. I was only a deal he chose not to refuse. Later, I would come to find that his son, who was studying the Law and the Prophets at the Jewish synagogue, needed a maidservant for his quarters.

Though I was not used for his personal services to fulfill his wanton desires, I was treated harshly and beaten on occasion to remind me of my place, or rather lack thereof. He knew my station and would endeavor to point out my sinful past as a way to express his holiness over my lowly estate. In time, I came to understand that his piousness had more to do with him and little to do with the God he claimed to know so much about. It was a hypocritical display of virtue. Still, I was reminded regularly of my ranking in the eyes of his self-righteousness. I was reminded by the subtle word, "Wasted."

Years passed and I grew accustomed to my daily routine as the maidservant of my master's son. However, a sense of freedom washed over me as I longed for a position in society that I never could obtain. I was a servant, a slave; bound to my master, yet I longed for a freedom I had never known. One day while performing my duties as my master was away at the synagogue, I happened upon an expensive alabaster box of precious ointment. I could hardly believe my eyes! I knew both the price of the box and the consequences of what would be if I were to take it into my possession.

This was my chance to purchase my freedom. She thought that if she stole the small box and sold it then she could use the money to purchase her own freedom. She knew that this was most logical answer to all of her problems, she even noted that her master would not notice its absence. It was fairly common for the master to bring home small, expensive ornaments after long trips to distant lands. I would surely liberate myself from this bondage once and for all!

Present Day

By this time some of the Pharisees in the room had recovered from the initial shock of this woman's presence and began whispering amongst themselves, criticizing her actions saying, "Wasted."

The rummaging around the room did not seem to bother her in the least. Her focus was devoted entirely to Him, Jesus. All at once she had found herself at his feet, worshipping, knowing full well she did not deserve to even be there. Simon was becoming impatient with the temptress. Jesus acknowledged Simon's thoughts and answered him saying, "Simon, I have a story for you." Caught a little off guard, but trying to maintain his clarity, Simon responded, "Yes, Master, go on."

"There was a certain man who had two debtors. One of them owed the man five hundred pence and the other owed him fifty. When both of them could not pay, the man forgave each one; completely wiping their slates clean." Jesus looked directly at Simon and said, "Tell me, Simon. Which debtor will love him more?"

It was obvious that Simon did not understand where this conversation was going. In his mind, it had nothing to do with the bigger situation at hand. But to remain composed, he replied.

"I suppose," He cleared his throat and glanced around the room before looking at Jesus again. "I suppose the one whose debt was larger." Jesus looked calmly at Simon and said, "You are correct."

Just as Simon was about to look around for the approval of his peers and his applaud for answering correctly, Jesus said his name again, but this time he was staring softly into the eyes of the woman at his feet.

"Simon?" Jesus did not break eye contact with her. "See this woman?" Jesus smiled down at her. "I came into your house and yet you did not bring me water to wash my feet," reaching over, He gently wiped a tear streaming down her cheek. "But she has washed my feet with her tears and wiped them with her hair." Simon was speechless. Jesus continued. "You did not receive me with a kiss, and yet this woman has not ceased to kiss my feet." Jesus kept wiping her tears away as she wept in silence. "You did not anoint my head with oil, but she has anointed my feet with ointment." Simon could not bring himself to look at Jesus. Jesus looked over at Simon and said his name once more. "Simon, I want you to know that her sins, which are many—they are forgiven. Because she has loved much." Jesus glanced at the woman with assurance and then focused his eyes on Simon again. "He who is forgiven little loves little."

Simon felt the conviction and dropped his head, unable to maintain eye contact with Jesus. Jesus then looked at the woman and took her hand. "Your sins are forgiven." Everyone in the room could not believe what they had just witnessed. Not only had Jesus accepted this wicked woman into His presence and ignored the fact that this was Simon's house and not His house, but now He was claiming to have forgiven her of all her sins, too? Though He knew the thoughts of every single individual in the room, Jesus eyes never left the woman kneeling before Him. As He stood to His feet, He carefully led her to stand. With compassion in His eyes and her hands still in His, He leaned down close to her face and said, "Your faith has saved you. Go in peace." Unable to comprehend all that had transpired in the last few moments, the woman could not bring herself to hold His gaze any longer. Overwhelmed, she still remembered the word that had haunted her from childhood to adulthood. She looked at the floor and whispered what she knew. “Wasted.” And Jesus, in all the glorious power and wonder of His majesty, lifted her chin. And as one last tear rolled silently down her cheek, He looked gently into her eyes and whispered His response. “Worthy.”* Story taken from Luke 7:36-50 and written with embellishment to enhance the imagination of the reader.

The woman in the story suffered judgment and condemnation from the religious leaders of the day, but received only love and forgiveness from Christ. The Bible says in Romans 8:1 “There is therefore now no condemnation to them which are in Christ Jesus, who walk not after the flesh, but the Spirit.” If you have truly repented from your sins and trusted in Christ alone by faith in His grace, according to God’s infallible Word, you will not be condemned. The Almighty God is now your Father and you are His child. Circumstances will be difficult. People will fail you. You will be persecuted if you are living in active obedience to Christ’s commands. Like the woman in the story, are you willing to suffer momentary persecution from others to gain the honor of being close to Christ and receiving forgiveness from Him alone?

Challenge

Revival and persecution go hand in hand. When Christians are persecuted then revival takes place! This is a result of a shift of our focus from ourselves to God. Persecution is currently happening all over the world. Some places have worse persecution than others, but as followers of Christ we should expect to be persecuted. When our focus is on God then it will not matter what happens to us, we will only strive to glorify God. The apostle Paul clearly says, "All that will live godly in Christ Jesus shall suffer persecution."[2] Are you being persecuted? If not, then by default, you are not living godly in Christ Jesus. It is really that simple. So you must decide today if Christ is worthy of your entire life. How much is following Christ worth to you? Would you be willing to die for the One who died for you? Are you content with merely calling yourself a "Christian" while neglecting to suffer persecution for His name's sake? To what extent are you willing to go so that others might see what you do and glorify the Father? I challenge you to become committed to sharing the Gospel of Jesus Christ with those who will spend an eternity in a real place called Hell without it. Do you accept the challenge?

The Next Step: The Outpouring of a Life in Christ

Let's get down to the point. I am going to be real with you. Jesus Christ says, "Enter ye in at the strait gate: for wide is the gate, and broad is the way, that leadeth to destruction, and many there be which go in thereat: because strait is the gate, and narrow is the way, which leadeth unto life, and few there be that find it."[3] This passage of scripture has been analyzed over and over again, but let me provide a very simplistic explanation for this verse as it has obviously confused many. Most people are going to Hell and very few are going to Heaven. The truth is difficult to accept, but according to this verse the majority of people in the world are not on their way to Heaven. This is sad and heartbreaking news. This is not a popular message. Nevertheless, this is a truth that needs to be proclaimed. It is vitally important that we completely grasp this concept in order for us to live in the way that is pleasing to our Lord and Savior Jesus Christ.

How should we, as Christ's followers, respond to this under-reported truth? Our entire motive for living should be centered on who Jesus is, why Jesus came, and how to make Jesus known to the world. We should begin to conduct our lives according to what Christ has told us to do instead of what we feel like doing. Although we may not always feel like obeying Christ, the sole purpose of our lives should be to obey Him. The more that we deny ourselves, the more we will naturally want to live our lives in submissive obedience for the One who gave us life.

Many things happen when we put aside our petty differences and simply believe God's Word enough to actually act upon the things we believe. When Christ becomes our life, the following things are true about us.

1. We reevaluate the motive behind all of our actions.
   When Christ truly becomes our life we will be more concerned with God's opinion of us than with what others think. We will evaluate the motive behind each and every action. We will do everything that Christ wants us to do because we love Him and He is our life. Only when we discover who we truly are in Christ are we at the point where we can obey Him with the right motivation. We should constantly strive to magnify Christ in everything that

we say and do. Every single thing we do in life ought to be done to the glory of God and the advancement of His Kingdom. Would the previous statement characterize your life? If not, determine to be different.

2. We refocus our attention on Christ alone.
When Christ becomes our life, our attention shifts from temporal to eternal. We will begin to exert our time, energy, and commitment into things that actually matter. We will begin to focus less on worldly pleasures and more of what glorifies the Father. We will begin listen to less of what pleases us and more of what pleases God. We will begin to say less of what we want to say and more of what will make a lasting impact in the lives of those around us. We will begin to think less about what we desire to dwell on and more about what Christ and His words instruct. Our entire mindset will begin to change into one of an eternal purpose. When Christ transforms one from death to life He creates in them an entirely new creation.[4]

3. We reconsider how we spend our time.
God has given one gift to every human being on the face of the earth- time. Each of us has been given a certain amount of time. Each of us has a choice of how to invest the time that we have been given by God. Time is a precious gift. Once it is gone, you cannot get it back. I have heard many older people tell me that they wished they had more time. People say "If only I had more time, I would have more money," "If only I had more time, I would have turned my back on sin and surrendered my life to Christ," "If I only had more time, I would have been a missionary serving God in another country." The phrase beginning with *if only* (you fill in the blank) has been said

> countless times throughout history. Perhaps you have said or wondered something along these lines before. I want you to know that it is not good to focus on what "might have been," but it is vital that you realize that what you do now is of great significance. Choose *right now* to invest the time you have been given by God for the advancement of His kingdom and magnification of His Son, Jesus Christ.

In light of what we have learned about making Christ our life, how can we adjust our lives to share the Gospel with those who have no life? After reading about who the Jesus Christ of the Bible is, what He has done, and what He offers those who abandon all to follow Him, are you willing to make Christ your life?

Thank You

Thank you for taking the time to read this book. Many long hours have gone into the writing and editing of this book all for the glory of The Lord and Savior Jesus Christ. We hope that this book has made an impact and you are now following Christ closer than ever before. My team and I would like to hear about any and all decisions that have been made through the reading of this book. If you would like to contact me please go to the book website: christislifebook.com or send an email at christislifebook@gmail.com.

About the Author

Nate Wilkerson is an eighteen year old, social media influencer with a reach of over 45,000. Early in his life, he surrendered to preach the Gospel around the world as a foreign, church planting missionary. He has traveled around the world from Mexico to China passionately preaching God's Word with a boldness few posses. Nate has lead hundreds to Christ and discipled dozens others through his social media platform and in person at both Christian and public school. He hopes to continue serving the Lord in full time capacity as long as there is breath in his lungs. Nate enjoys traveling, preaching, writing, helping those in need, practicing and playing various sports in his free time. Nate professes himself to be "a nobody who exists to tell everybody about Somebody who can forgive anybody." Nate wants CHRIST to be magnified in Him through life and death, and continuously says "He must increase, but I must decrease".

Notes

PURPOSE CHAPTER 1

1 Joshua 6:18
2 Hebrews 11:6
3 Philippians 2:10

PRIORITIES CHAPTER 2

1 John 4:8
2 Revelation 3:17

PERSPECTIVE CHAPTER 3

1 Acts 17:6
2 1 John 1:9
3 2 Kings 6:14
4 2 Kings 6:16
5 1 John 4:4
6 2 Kings 6:22
7 John 9:3
8 1 Peter 2:9
9 Genesis 1:31

PROBLEMS CHAPTER 4

1 Hebrews 13:8

2 1 Corinthians 6:19-20

PATIENCE CHAPTER 5

1 Mark 16:15
2. Mark 16:15
3. Genesis 17:4
4. Genesis 12:7
5. Genesis 12:15
6. Genesis 12:16
7. Hebrews 11:25
8. Matthew 7:7-11
9. Genesis 12:17
10. 1 Corinthians 13:4
11. Proverbs 22:1

PURITY CHAPTER 6

1. Matthew 5:48
2. Ephesians 2:2-3
3. Romans 3:23
4. 1 John 1:9
5. Luke 16:13
6. Matthew 5:28
7. 1 John 1:9

PRAYER CHAPTER 7

1. 2 Samuel 7:18
2. Mark 11:25
3. 1 Chronicles 6:13; Daniel 6:10; Luke 22:41; Acts 7:60, 9:40, 20:36, 21:5; Ephesians 3:14
4. Matthew 26:39; Mark 14:35
5. 1 Timothy 2:8
6. Romans 5:6-12
7. Ephesians 2:18-22
8. Psalms 51:12

PRICE CHAPTER 8

1. Matthew 4:19
2. 1 Kings 18:21
3. 1 Corinthians 6:19-20
4. John 14:6
5. Ephesians 2:8-9
6. 2 Corinthians 5:17
7. Matthew 5:10-12
8. Luke 9:57-62
9. Psalms 143:10
10. Mark 10:18
11. Job 1:1
12. Job 1:3
13. Isaiah 55:8-9
14. Judges 16:30
15. Genesis 39:9
16. Genesis 39:21
17. 1 Peter 5:6
18. 1 Corinthians 10:13

PERSECUTION CHAPTER 9

1. Acts 8:3
2. 2 Timothy 3:12
3. Matthew 7:13-14
4. 2 Corinthians 5:17

Works Cited

Arterburn, Stephen, Fred Stoeker, and Mike Yorkey. *Every Young Man's Battle: Strategies for Victory in the Real World of Sexual Temptation.* Colorado Springs, CO: WaterBrook, 2009. Print.

Foxe, John, and Harold J. Chadwick. *The New Foxe's Book of Martyrs 2001.* Gainesville, FL: Bridge-Logos, 2001. Print.

Harris, Joshua. *I Kissed Dating Goodbye.* Sisters, Or: Multnomah, 2003. Print.

Jones, Richard, bookseller, Dorman Newman, Thomas Daniel, and Thomas Ratcliffe. The Excellency of the Pen And Pencil: Exemplifying the Uses of Them In the Most Exquisite And Mysterious Arts of Drawing, Etching, Engraving, Limning, Painting In Oyl, Washing of Maps & Pictures, Also the Way to Cleanse Any Old Painting, And Preserve the Colours : Collected From the Writings of the Ablest Masters, Both Antient And Modern, As Albert Durer, P. Lomantius, And Divers Others : Furnished With Divers Cuts In Copper, Being Copied From the Best Masters, And Here Inserted for Examples for the Learner to Practice by ... London:

Printed by Thomas Ratcliff and Thomas Daniel, for Dorman Newman and Richard Jones ..., 1668.

Knight, Kevin. "Prescription against Heretics." *CHURCH FATHERS: The Prescription Against Heretics (Tertullian).* New Advent, 11 Mar. 2009. Web. 25 Oct. 2016.

Lewis, C. S. *The Weight of Glory: And Other Addresses.* San Francisco: HarperSanFrancisco, 2005. Print.

Ludy, Eric, and Leslie Ludy. *When God Writes Your Love Story: The Ultimate Guide to Guy/girl Relationships.* Colorado Springs, CO: Multnomah, 2009. Print.

Mischel, Walter, Ebbe B. Ebbesen, and Antonette Raskoff Zeiss. "Cognitive and Attentional Mechanisms in Delay of Gratification." *Journal of Personality and Social Psychology* 21.2 (1972): 204-18. Web.

"5 facts about prayer." Pew Research Center, Washington, D.C. 2014. http://www.pewresearch.org/fact-tank/2016/05/04/5-facts-about-prayer/#, December 12, 2016.

"riotous." Merriam-Webster.com. Merriam-Webster, 2017. Web. 9 April 2017.

Printed in the United States
By Bookmasters